This book belongs to:

About the Author

ALED JONES has had an extraordinary career over the past four decades. He is the original crossover star and has sung for the Pope and the Royal Family, has received an MBE, released over 40 albums with over 10 million album sales and counting, and has over 40 Silver, Gold and Platinum Discs. He continues to perform all over the world and will be touring the UK and Australia in 2026.

He is the main presenter on the BBC's *Songs of Praise* programme and presents the most listened to radio shows on Classic FM on Saturday and Sunday mornings.

Aled's
Book of
Blessings
for
2026

ALED JONES

HODDER &
STOUGHTON

First published in Great Britain by Hodder Faith in 2025
An imprint of John Murray Press

1

Copyright © Aled Jones 2025

A CIP catalogue record for this title is available from the British Library

Hardback ISBN 978 1 399 82109 4
ebook ISBN 978 1 399 82110 0

Typeset in Garamond Premier Pro

Printed and bound in Great Britain by Clays Ltd, Elcograf S.p.A.

John Murray Press policy is to use papers that are natural, renewable
and recyclable products and made from wood grown in sustainable forests.
The logging and manufacturing processes are expected to conform to
the environmental regulations of the country of origin.

Carmelite House
50 Victoria Embankment
London EC4Y 0DZ

www.hodderfaith.com

John Murray Press, part of Hodder & Stoughton Limited
An Hachette UK company

The authorised representative in the EEA is Hachette Ireland, 8 Castlecourt
Centre, Dublin 15, D15 XTP3, Ireland (email: info@hbgi.ie)

For Carmel, one of life's greatest blessings.
The voice of reason and love.

CONTENTS

INTRODUCTION

Why Do We Need Blessings?

B lessings play an essential role in our lives, offering peace, protection and positivity, whether spiritual, religious or simply well-wishes from others. Many believe blessings bring divine favour, guidance and strength. In faiths like Christianity, Islam, Hinduism and Buddhism, they are seen as powerful forces shaping life's journey. Beyond religion, blessings from our elders, parents and mentors carry deep respect and encouragement. In many cultures, they mark life's biggest moments like marriage, new beginnings or personal milestones, offering confidence, motivation and inner peace. Giving blessings to others also creates a cycle of goodwill, reminding us that kindness and affirmation are transformative forces.

Despite all our technological advancements, blessings remain as important today as ever, perhaps even more so. In a fast-paced world filled with uncertainty and stress, they provide emotional strength, moral guidance and a sense of spiritual connection. They preserve cultural traditions and reinforce values like kindness, gratitude and hope. At a time when digital interactions dominate, blessings serve as a reminder of real human warmth and support.

As we grow older, we begin to appreciate blessings more deeply. Life teaches us resilience and appreciation, revealing how much the support of family, mentors and spiritual sources truly matters. Success is rarely a solo journey; it's often shaped by the encouragement and blessings of others. Ageing also brings a deeper connection to spirituality and tradition, making us more mindful of the wisdom passed down through generations. Beyond receiving blessings, we begin to take joy in giving them, offering encouragement and well-wishes to others, and seeing how a few kind words can uplift someone's spirit.

While science may not prove the supernatural power of blessings, research shows that prayer, meditation and positive affirmations reduce stress, improve mental health and can even boost healing. In my own journey, I have seen first-hand the impact of blessings, both in my daily life and in my work as a celebrant.

Who knew that a chance encounter would lead me down this path? It all began when someone told me that my version of 'You Raise Me Up' was the most requested song in UK crematoriums. That revelation moved me deeply. Knowing that my voice was part of something so personal and meaningful inspired me to explore a new calling. Becoming a celebrant has been one of the most fulfilling and nerve-racking roles of my life. Whether officiating at a wedding or a funeral, I am honoured to be part of life's most significant moments. I take this responsibility seriously and strive to make each ceremony perfect. Compared to this, singing and presenting feel easy!

Many people shared how my first *Everyday Blessings* book brought them comfort, and I have been touched by their stories. A common practice among readers is to turn immediately to the blessing on their birth date. So many have told me that the words resonated deeply, as if written just for them. Perhaps that is a case of a higher power at work.

More Than Blessings

For this collection, I have added another layer of personal meaning. At the start of each month, I share reflections on some of the classical composers and pieces that have shaped my life. Music has always been a guiding force for me, and I hope these insights inspire you to explore these timeless works for yourselves.

You'll also notice a number of blank boxes with prompts throughout the book – they are there on purpose! If inspiration strikes, I encourage you to jot down your own thoughts, feelings, or even compose a blessing of your own. By recording your emotions and reflections, you create a personal keepsake of your mindset during 2026.

I recommend starting each day with a blessing. Take a moment to read it, absorb it and let it guide your thoughts. Try to keep distractions to a minimum for maximum benefit. While I can't promise a revelation each day, if a single blessing makes you pause, smile or reflect for even a few seconds, that's already better than doom-scrolling on social media.

I ended the introduction to my first *Everyday Blessings* book with these words, and I believe they remain just as relevant today:

I hope the words of wisdom in this book transport you somewhere else and offer comfort and hope in equal measure. Whether you believe in God, follow a particular faith, or simply want to reconnect with our shared humanity across the ages, these blessings and inspirational thoughts are just the tonic.

Please enjoy!

Aled

January

Wolfgang Amadeus Mozart –
Requiem in D minor, K. 626

'I pay no attention whatever to anybody's praise
or blame. I simply follow my own feelings.'

WOLFGANG AMADEUS MOZART

Picture the scene: it's a chilly January evening in Salzburg. Leopold Mozart, a musician, is pacing the floors of his flat. His wife, Maria Anna, is in labour and about to give birth. Even though this was the seventh time she had been through childbirth, Leopold and his wife had only one surviving child, a girl of four. You can imagine what Leopold and Maria Anna were feeling when, at around eight o'clock that evening, Maria Anna gave birth to a healthy baby boy, Johannes Chrysostomus Wolfgangus Theophilus Mozart.

Baby Mozart became a 'child star'. It's a title that was occasionally bestowed on a certain Welshman who I know very well! (Just for the record, I hated it – it always makes me think of tap shoes and ringlets.) Where I was just a kid with a nice voice and, some would say, impeccable phrasing, Mozart really was a star from a very, very early age. Only three days before his fifth birthday, taught by his violinist father, he learnt to play his first piece of music. By the age of six he was composing and travelling all over Europe playing music for anyone who would listen. The royals loved him, and he had many contacts with the aristocracy. His touring schedule made current pop goddess Taylor Swift look lazy; it was relentless and I can't begin to imagine what it was like for him. To give you an idea about how many countries he visited, it's been said that Mozart could speak fifteen languages! Yet once the hubbub surrounding his touring-child-prodigy-circus-act had died down, Mozart's miraculous genius was largely misunderstood and unappreciated.

Throughout his brief but prolific career, Mozart composed over 600 works, including symphonies, operas, chamber music and choral works, and it's been said that he tapped the source from which all music flows. My personal favourite piece of his, and one which has made a huge impact on my life, is his *Requiem*. It's a piece of music that shoots straight to my heart and soul and mines the depths of so many human emotions.

A requiem focuses our minds to take stock and remember the death and resurrection of Christ. The service also gives space to reflect on hope and the new life Jesus brings, even in the face of death. Mozart's *Requiem* has captivated audiences for centuries, not only for its profound beauty but also for the mystique and drama surrounding its origins. A widely circulated yet exaggerated tale suggests a mysterious stranger commissioned the piece in secret under the cover of night. In reality, the *Requiem* was commissioned by Count Franz von Walsegg, a wealthy nobleman known for having composers write works that he would later claim as his own. While the true backstory lacks the flair of legend, it's no less intriguing.

Tragically, Mozart did not live to finish it. He passed away on 5 December 1791, at the age of thirty-five, leaving some sections completed, others sketched and portions untouched. His pupil, Franz Xaver Süssmayr, later undertook the task of completing it. But despite its fragmented creation, the *Requiem* stands as a towering masterpiece that showcases Mozart's exceptional genius.

Mozart's music has been a source of comfort and inspiration for me, whether during moments of triumph or personal struggle. One particular occasion, that I'm not too proud to recall, was during my time at David Hughes Comprehensive School in North Wales. I was a teenager who had just experienced the raw emotion of my 'first true love' breaking up with me and I was distraught. Like a guardian angel, my mother came into my room and, obviously aware of my lack of sodium from the crying, presented me with a bowl of salted popcorn! She dispatched a few words of wisdom and then handed me two vinyl recordings. One was Andy Williams' *Greatest Hits* and the other was a recording of Mozart's *Requiem*. As much as I enjoyed the Andy Williams offering, Mozart's album, which I knew nothing about, had a profound effect on me. I'm not ashamed to say I listened from start to finish with tears welling in my eyes and a sea of emotions swirling inside. In the space of an hour my emotional rollercoaster took me from sadness and grief, anger and frustration, confusion and uncertainty, nostalgia and loneliness to, finally, hope and liberation – a free therapy session in the comfort of my own room. The *Requiem* became my go-to in those uncertain moments throughout adolescence. I'm living proof that Mozart's *Requiem* has the power to heal.

In my opinion, Mozart's own personality shines through his music. He was a complex character with boundless energy and a thirst for fun and adventure. Much of his music has a 'playful' nature, which I love, often evoking joy, sorrow, passion and serenity – sometimes all within the one piece. This is very true of his *Requiem*; he manages to capture both the sorrows and triumphs of life and death.

It is believed that Mozart wrote only the first eight bars of the 'Lacrimosa' section of the *Requiem* before he died. 'Lacrimosa' means 'tearful' or 'weeping' in Latin. Talk about drama – no wonder they made his life story into a film! Some have speculated that, aware of his own imminent death, Mozart poured his feelings into the 'Lacrimosa', composing not only for the departed but also as a means of confronting his own mortality. There is definitely a sense of heightened drama and a profound sadness in this section and, call me an old sentimental, but I always think of Mozart confronting his own mortality at bar eight when I play the piece. What a loss to the world it was that he died so young.

The *Requiem*'s mournful tone and solemn themes often lead people to reflect on personal experiences of loss and the fragility of existence. But, for me, the work also offers a cathartic release, channelling grief into a shared expression of beauty and hope. The grandeur of the piece, with its sweeping choral passages, connects listeners to something greater than themselves. It is also a very intimate piece, and in my bedroom, back in the day, it was as if Mozart was dictating the piece straight to my soul.

In many ways, the *Requiem* can be seen as a musical representation of mourning and an acknowledgement of life's transience. Much like the passage from one year to the next, it marks an end while also offering the potential for renewal. January, the first month of the brand-new year, symbolises new beginnings and the promise of fresh starts. It's a time for reflection on the past and anticipation of what lies ahead.

Along with the flurry of activity that comes from New Year's resolutions, there is wisdom also in making space to ask: What do I *not* want to take into this new year? What do I need to say goodbye to as I step into this new beginning?

A requiem creates an atmosphere of reverence and calm, speaking to the spaces left by those who have departed.

This stillness mirrors January's quiet, reflective mood. The cold, often barren, landscapes of winter foster introspection and a slower pace of life. In this way, both the Mozart's *Requiem* and the season share a sense of solemnity and renewal; both invite us to pause, reflect and find meaning in times of transition.

Personal reflection often deepens the impact of Mozart's *Requiem* for me. I am reminded of the passing of my beloved dog, Cybi, whose gentle spirit and boundless energy brought immense comfort and joy to my family. Each January, I pause to honour his memory and carry forward his zest for life. This act of remembrance mirrors the emotional journey of listening to the *Requiem* – a moment to grieve, reflect and find inspiration in the resilience of the human (and, in my case, animal) spirit. Cybi was the heart and soul of our family for the short time he was with us. He was a fluffy white cloud of joy, kindness, positivity and calm. When he passed away in January, he left a huge hole in our house and in our lives, but he also taught us all so many invaluable lessons that I try to take with me through life. He seemed to live life 'just for today', embracing each new day with an open heart and full of zest. You can learn from the past, but you can't bring it back, and you should never dwell on it! I can very easily get bogged

down in the bleak and barren feeling that January instils in me, but when this happens, nowadays, I take a time out and with coffee in hand, I think of Cybi and his 'attitude of gratitude'. January, after all, carries the promise of renewal and, just like Mozart's *Requiem*, it's a prelude to the hope of spring to come.

1 January: *New Year's Day*

Focus on your strengths, not your weaknesses. Focus on your character, not your reputation. Focus on your blessings, not your misfortunes.

ROY T. BENNETT, *The Light in the Heart*

2 January

The manner of giving is worth more than the gift.

PIERRE CORNEILLE, *The Liar*

3 January

Almost all our misfortunes in life come from the wrong notions we have about the things that happen to us. To know men thoroughly, to judge events sanely, is, therefore, a great step towards happiness.

STENDHAL, 10 December 1801,
The Private Diaries of Stendhal

4 January

To go wrong in one's own way is better than to go right in someone else's.

FYODOR DOSTOEVSKY, *Crime and Punishment*

5 January: *Twelfth Night*

When God takes out the trash, don't go digging back through it. Trust Him.

AMAKA IMANI NKOSAZANA, *Heart Crush*

6 January: *Epiphany*

Half our mistakes in life arise from feeling where we ought to think, and thinking where we ought to feel.

JOHN CHURTON COLLINS

7 January: *Orthodox Christmas Day*

Begin at once to live, and count each separate day as a separate life.

SENECA, *Letters to Lucilius*

As you start this new year, what possibilities do you think 2026 might hold?

8 January

Love is a naked child: do you think he has pockets for money?

OVID, *The Loves*

9 January

Be still, my soul. The Lord is on thy side.
Bear patiently the cross of grief or pain.
Leave to thy God to order and provide.
In ev'ry change He faithful will remain.
Be still, my soul. Thy best, thy heav'nly friend
Through thorny ways leads to a joyful end.

KATHARINA VON SCHLEGEL,
'Be Still, My Soul', 1752

10 January

You only live once, but if you do it right, once is enough.

MAE WEST

11 January

What you lost is nothing compared to what the Lord has in store for you. Pray and claim your blessings from the Almighty God.

GIFT GUGU MONA,
Prayer: An Antidote for the Inner Man

12 January

My arms are wide open to all of the blessings that are coming my way. I fully accept them with immense gratitude.

ROBIN S. BAKER

What are you thankful for today?

13 January

Try and leave this world a little better than you found it, and when your turn comes to die, you can die happy in feeling that at any rate, you have not wasted your time but have done your best.

ROBERT BADEN-POWELL,
'Last Message to Scouts', 1941

14 January

In order to carry a positive action we must develop here a positive vision.

DALAI LAMA XIV

15 January

No matter what you're going through, there's a light at the end of the tunnel and it may seem hard to get to it but you can do it and just keep working towards it and you'll find the positive side of things.

DEMI LOVATO

16 January

Trust in dreams, for in them is hidden the gate to eternity.

KAHLIL GIBRAN, *The Prophet*

17 January

Instead of hating, I have chosen to forgive and spend all of my positive energy on changing the world.

CAMRYN MANHEIM

18 January: *World Religion Day*

In my deepest, darkest moments, what really got me through was a prayer. Sometimes my prayer was 'Help me.' Sometimes a prayer was 'Thank you.' What I've discovered is that intimate connection and communication with my creator will always get me through because I know my support, my help, is just a prayer away.

IYANLA VANZANT on 'Tell me More', *NRP Music*, 2011

19 January

A lot of things are going to happen that you can't necessarily control all the time, but you can control what you do after it happens. So that's what I try to do, keep my head up, keep moving forward, stay positive and just work hard.

LONZO BALL

What are the things to remember today that you cannot control?

20 January

Believe that life is worth living and your belief will help create the fact.

WILLIAM JAMES, 'Is Life Worth Living',
Harvard University Address, May 1895

21 January

When you arise in the morning, think of what a precious privilege it is to be alive – to breathe, to think, to enjoy, to love.

MARCUS AURELIUS, *Meditations*

22 January

It is not death that a man should fear, but he should fear never beginning to live.

MARCUS AURELIUS, *Meditations*

23 January

God, grant me the serenity to accept the things
I cannot change, the courage to change the things I can,
and the wisdom to know the difference.

REINHOLD NIEBUHR, 'Serenity Prayer'

24 January

Live on in your blessings, your destiny's been won.
But ours calls us on from one ordeal to the next.

VIRGIL, The Aeneid

25 January: *Burns Night*

Anyone can hold the helm when the sea is calm.

PUBLILIUS SYRUS, *Sententiae*

26 January

There is nothing permanent except change.

HERACLITUS, *Fragments*

27 January: *Holocaust Memorial Day*

It is only with true love and compassion that we can begin to mend what is broken in the world. It is these two blessed things that can begin to heal all broken hearts.

STEVE MARABOLI, *Life, the Truth, and Being Free*

28 January

In life, our first job is this, to divide and distinguish things into two categories: externals I cannot control, but the choices I make with regard to them I do control. Where will I find good and bad? In me, in my choices.

EPICTETUS, *Discourses*

29 January

What is defeat? Nothing but education. Nothing
but the first steps to something better.

WENDELL PHILLIPS, 'Harper's Ferry', 1859

30 January

If you falter in a time of trouble,
how small is your strength!

Proverbs 24:10

31 January

When your time comes to die, be not like those whose
hearts are filled with fear of death, so that when their
time comes they weep and pray for a little more time to
live their lives over again in a different way. Sing your
death song, and die like a hero going home.

TECUMSEH

Notes for January

February

George Frideric Handel –
Jephtha

'I should be sorry if I only entertained them.
I wish to make them better.'

GEORGE FRIDERIC HANDEL

I'm not kidding when I say that the composer George Frideric Handel played a part in launching my child career. He wasn't there accompanying or conducting me at the time (because he was born in 1685!), but he composed the music that introduced me to the world. And for that I'm eternally grateful – cheers Handel!

Even though many people believe that the Christmas song 'Walking in the Air' started everything for me, it was, in fact, Handel's oratorio (that is, a large-scale musical composition for orchestra, choir and soloists) *Jephtha*. I was twelve years old and had been booked to sing the small part of the Angel in the production, which was being performed at St David's Hall in Cardiff. I lived at the time in North Wales and had never been to Cardiff, which is in the South. My first professional engagement was quite a big event: I was to share the stage with some very prominent classical singers, and we were all to be accompanied by the BBC Welsh Symphony Orchestra and conducted by the legendary Sir Neville Marriner. The concert was also being broadcast live on BBC Radio 3. So, no pressure!

To be fair, I had the easiest part. I'd been told just to learn the recit, which is a short narrative piece of singing that advances the plot. The main 'showy' aria usually follows the recit and I had specifically been told that I wouldn't be singing the aria because I was so young and there were strict time constraints due to the BBC broadcast.

While learning and rehearsing my part, though, my teachers had also made me learn the aria, just for the experience. It was a very flamboyant song and technically difficult, but I loved it. Singing Handel's music was as easy as breathing for me. It all felt so effortless, almost as if he had written the piece especially for me! Thank goodness I did learn the aria, because on the morning of the piano rehearsal with Sir Neville, the pianist just carried on playing after the recit, and I just carried on singing! At the end of the song Sir Neville turned to all in the room and exclaimed: 'This aria must go into the performance!' The role of the Angel had suddenly gone from 'minor to major!'

The next evening, I stood in St David's Hall in Cardiff in front of 2,000 people, sporting a ridiculously large home-made velvet bow tie which mum had created herself. Mum and dad were in the audience, probably more nervous than I was. Mum had a habit of mouthing the words with me 'realtime' during a performance and had done this ever since I performed publicly for the first time (that auspicious occasion was the primary school nativity where I played Shepherd No. 2). It meant that poor mum was usually exhausted by the end of the performance. Dad, on the other hand, would block everything out and just bite his fingernails. Now, as I look back on this particular performance, my professional debut, it must have been such a life-changing event for my parents too – their little boy was totally exposed on the big stage and under so much pressure; and as parents they couldn't do anything to help. (On a separate note, I've been there myself now, with my daughter, who is an actress. The feeling of helplessness is crippling!) But my parents needn't have worried. Even though there were over a hundred musicians assembled on stage, I was in a world of my own – it was just me, Neville Marriner and Handel's glorious music. And then, just like that, it was over. Cries of 'Bravo!' and endless curtain calls followed and, in that moment, a little chorister from North Wales' life changed for ever.

My first experience of Handel's composing brilliance came as a fresh-faced chorister at Bangor Cathedral. Excitement levels reached fever pitch when it was announced that we were going to be heading to Germany on a choir trip. I was only ten years old and the furthest from home I'd ever been was Chester Zoo, which was about an hour away, along the A55!

To raise some much-needed funds to subsidise the trip, it was decided that we would put on a benefit concert in the largest hall at Bangor University. Even though we were used to singing the psalms, hymns and anthems at the Cathedral, this felt like a big step up. Our choirmaster added to the already growing nerves by making us learn and perform Handel's anthem 'Zadok the Priest', especially for the concert. It's the most famous of Handel's coronation anthems and was composed for King George II of England in 1727; it has been performed at every coronation since. It is also the first piece of music that was played on the radio station Classic FM when it launched in 1992, and has even made it into popular culture as the football Champions League theme tune.

To say that our performance of this iconic masterpiece was substandard would be the understatement of the century and the memory of this spectacular failure will remain with me always. Nerves got the better of us and many of the younger choristers just froze mid-performance and stopped singing. But I didn't – I carried on ploughing through the piece, even though all attempts at subtlety and beauty had disappeared.

It was survival of the fittest. I got the impression even back then that you needed to be a larger-than-life character to perform his music. Maybe that's because he was a larger-than-life composer.

It's not just me who loves Handel's music. Composer Ludwig van Beethoven is quoted as saying: 'Handel is the greatest composer who ever lived. I would uncover my head and kneel down on his grave.' Also, Wolfgang Amadeus Mozart, who, let's face it, knew a thing or two about writing, remarked: 'Handel understands effect better than any of us. When he chooses, he strikes like a thunderbolt.' We're lucky he wrote any music at all, because his father wanted young Handel to be a lawyer and didn't like music in the house. Thankfully he never realised that young Handel used to sneak up to the loft to practise on his harpsichord in secret.

Love, in its many forms, is a recurring theme in Handel's music, reflected not only in romantic passion but also in the broader sense of compassion, divine devotion and the bonds between humanity, across ages and societies. His music has joy and ecstasy as well as sorrow and struggle. Maybe that is why his music is so often performed or played at weddings, celebrations and commemorations. Handel's operas are particularly rich in their exploration of romantic love. Within these dramatic works, characters grapple with the challenges, triumphs and heartbreaks of love. Handel's ability to create vivid characterisations through music allows us to empathise with their joys and struggles. The arias (songs), often a vehicle for the most intense emotional expression, give voice to the characters' innermost feelings.

Beyond romantic love, Handel's music often explores the themes of compassion and selfless love. His sacred works, including his celebrated oratorios, like *Jephtha* which gave me my big break, reflect a deep sense of devotion and spiritual love. When I sing these pieces, I feel a connection with a higher power, something far greater than myself. The choral sections, in particular, evoke a sense of communal worship and shared faith, which swell the heart, underscoring the idea that love is both an individual and a collective experience.

Nothing does this better than his oratorio *Messiah*. I have sung it many times, and am always affected by its profound emotional depth. It is a masterful composition, and, quite rightly, enjoys an enduring popularity. Its majestic choruses, especially the 'Hallelujah Chorus', are iconic, while its blend of spiritual themes and dramatic music makes it a timeless masterpiece. There is a tradition for the audience to stand during the 'Hallelujah Chorus': legend has it that during the London premiere of Handel's *Messiah*, King George II was so moved by it that he actually stood up and everyone else followed suit so as not to be seated in the King's presence. In truth, though, there is no evidence to suggest that the King even attended the premiere, but it's a good story, isn't it? At any rate, the work's universal appeal lies in its ability to inspire awe and joy, transcending religious and cultural boundaries, whether you're seated or standing!

Handel's melodies are elegant and memorable, designed to highlight the voice's natural qualities. These melodies often sit well within the range of the human voice, making them so pleasing and comfortable to sing. You can display virtuosity without excessive strain. The composer's music typically has a clear and logical structure, often based on repetition. We singers are encouraged to add our own ornaments and embellishments (extra notes added to the original melody), giving us the opportunity to showcase our technical skill and creativity while making the music our own. I adored being allowed to put a bit of myself into Handel's music, and very quickly I learnt that less is more. In the early days, while rehearsing with my teachers round our big black upright piano, I'd challenge myself to make the embellishments as tricky and flashy as possible; it was a perfect opportunity to show what my voice could do. My first attempt was in a favourite aria of mine, 'Where'er You Walk'. I littered the repeated last verse with as many notes as possible – poor Handel would have turned in his grave.

Singing Handel's music is so rewarding. He was a master of setting text to music, capturing the emotions and nuances of the lyrics. His compositions often align beautifully with the natural flow of the words, making it easier for us singers to connect emotionally and convey meaning to the audience. In the case of 'Ombra Mai Fu', another of my favourite Handel arias, the words are merely an ode to a plane tree, under whose shade the singer finds peace and comfort. Not groundbreaking stuff! But add into the mix the composer's very long sweeping musical phrases, which extend high and low in the vocal register, and the piece becomes something utterly sublime. On paper the song may look simple, but take it from me, it requires lungs of steel and total vocal control. To sing it well is a real undertaking, but when one does get it right, it's definitely a heaven on earth moment.

Handel's pieces have a timeless quality and speak to me deeply, as they have to others for generations. His music captures the essence of human emotion in a way that feels as relevant today as it did centuries ago. Whether experienced in a grand concert hall in Cardiff or a more intimate setting, Handel's music can touch the heart and stir the soul, not just of the audience but of the performer too.

1 February

By all means, marry. If you get a good wife, you'll become happy; if you get a bad one, you'll become a philosopher.

SOCRATES

2 February: *Groundhog Day*

The love of family and the admiration of friends is much more important than wealth and privilege.

CHARLES KURALT

3 February

To love oneself is the beginning of a lifelong romance.

OSCAR WILDE, An Ideal Husband

4 February: *World Cancer Day*

It's not that you should never love something
    so much that it can control you.
It's that you need to love something that much so
    you can never be controlled.
It's not a weakness.
It's your best strength.

PATRICK NESS, *The Ask and the Answer*

5 February

There are no strangers here; only friends you haven't
yet met.

WILLIAM BUTLER YEATS

Who are the friends you are most
thankful for?

6 February: *Winter Olympics, Italy*

O Lord that lends me life,
Lend me a heart replete with thankfulness!

WILLIAM SHAKESPEARE,
Henry VI, Part 2

7 February

True love is not a strong, fiery, impetuous passion.
It is, on the contrary, an element calm and deep.
It looks beyond mere externals, and is attracted by
qualities alone. It is wise and discriminating, and
its devotion is real and abiding.

ELLEN G. WHITE, *Letters to Young Lovers*

8 February

With the new day comes new strength and new thoughts.

ELEANOR ROOSEVELT in 'My Day', 8 January 1936

9 February

A real friend is one who walks in when the rest of the world walks out.

WALTER WINCHELL, *On Broadway*

10 February

Let's practice motivation and love, not discrimination and hate.

ZENDAYA

11 February

A single rose can be my garden . . . a single friend, my world.

LEO BUSCAGLIA

12 February

The only way to have a friend is to be one.

RALPH WALDO EMERSON, 'Friendship'

Take a moment to think how you could
be a good friend today.

13 February

The real act of marriage takes place in the heart, not in the ballroom or church or synagogue. It's a choice you make – not just on your wedding day, but over and over again – and that choice is reflected in the way you treat your husband or wife.

BARBARA DE ANGELIS

14 February: *St Valentine's Day*

Love in the making sees faults; love in the fulfillment sees none. Seeing faults is like cutting love into pieces, murdering love.

PAPA RAMDAS

15 February: *Singles Awareness Day*

When the heart of your heart opens, you can take deep pleasure in the company of the people around you . . . When you are open to the beauty, mystery, and grandeur of ordinary existence, you 'get it' that it always has been beautiful, mysterious, and grand and always will be.

TIMOTHY RAY MILLER

16 February

Lots of people want to ride with you in the limo, but what you want is someone who will take the bus with you when the limo breaks down.

OPRAH WINFREY

17 February: *Pancake Day (Shrove Tuesday)*

Shine your soul with the same egoless humility as the rainbow and no matter where you go in this world or the next, love will find you, attend you, and bless you.

ABERJHANI, *Journey through the Power of the Rainbow*

18 February: *Ash Wednesday*

Walking with a friend in the dark is better than walking alone in the light.

HELEN KELLER

19 February

If you treat people as they are, they will become worse.
If you treat them as they could be, they will become better.
If we treat people as if they were what they ought to be,
we help them become what they are capable of becoming.

JOHANN WOLFGANG VON GOETHE

20 February

Weddings are important because they celebrate life and possibility.

ANNE HATHAWAY
in *Interview Magazine*

21 February

There is nothing in the world so irresistibly contagious as laughter and good humour.

CHARLES DICKENS, *A Christmas Carol*

22 February: *First Sunday of Lent*

Work is love made visible. And if you cannot work with love but only with distaste, it is better that you should leave your work and sit at the gate of the temple and take alms of those who work with joy.

KAHLIL GIBRAN, *The Prophet*

23 February

I have learned that to be with those I like
is enough.

WALT WHITMAN, *Leaves of Grass*

Who would you like to spend more time with this year?

24 February

One of the most beautiful qualities of true friendship
is to understand and to be understood.

SENECA

25 February

Getting married, for me, was the best thing I ever
did. I was suddenly beset with an immense sense of
release, that we have something more important than
our separate selves, and that is the marriage. There's
immense happiness that can come from working
towards that.

NICK CAVE

26 February

In everyone's life, at some time, our inner fire goes out. It is then burst into flame by an encounter with another human being. We should all be thankful for those people who rekindle the inner spirit.

ALBERT SCHWEITZER

27 February

Character is like a tree and reputation like its shadow. The shadow is what we think of it; the tree is the real thing.

ABRAHAM LINCOLN

28 February

My definition of a friend is somebody who adores you even though they know the things you're most ashamed of.

JODIE FOSTER

Notes for February

March

J.S. Bach / Charles Gounod – 'Ave Maria'

'I was obliged to be industrious. Whoever is equally
industrious will succeed just as well.'

JOHANN SEBASTIAN BACH

The composer Johann Sebastian Bach didn't leave behind
many personal writings or notable quotes, but the one
above does reflect his disciplined work ethic. It could also
easily describe his life as a father of twenty children – I can't
begin to get my head around what that must have been like.
Just imagine bath time (I'd rather not!).

J.S. Bach's own childhood was rather tough. He was born
in the year 1685, in Eisenach, Germany, into a highly musical
family, and he was trained in violin, organ and composition

from an early age. Orphaned by the age of ten, he was raised by his older brother, Johann Christoph Bach, who thankfully further nurtured his musical talent. Though J.S. Bach's music was largely forgotten after his death, the composer Felix Mendelssohn revived interest in his works in the nineteenth century, cementing Bach's legacy as a musical genius. He is now regarded as one of the greatest composers of all time.

Charles Gounod was born in Paris in the year 1818, some sixty-eight years after Bach's death. He is best known for his operas and sacred music. Like Bach, he was born into an artistic family and studied at the Paris Conservatoire, winning the prestigious Prix de Rome in 1839, which allowed him to study in Italy.

Gounod's 'Ave Maria', a reimagining of one of Bach's preludes, was my first introduction to Gounod's music, and I loved his collaboration with Bach. The 'Ave Maria' ('Hail Mary') is a Catholic prayer to the Blessed Virgin Mary, asking for her intercession on behalf of sinners. The prayer has been set to music by many composers over the years and nowadays I must have at least a dozen versions by different composers in my repertoire. Back when I was a child, I either sang Schubert's setting or Bach/Gounod's version. The latter became my favourite: it is a perfect piece for a boy soprano, really letting you show off the clarity, purity and smooth legato of your singing.

I loved the way the melody floated effortlessly in my range. The long, sustained phrases help showcase the natural brilliance and innocence of a young voice, while the piece isn't overly demanding in terms of vocal agility, so you can focus on phrasing, dynamics and emotion. The combination of Bach's flowing harmony and Gounod's soaring melody creates a piece that feels both heavenly and soothing. Even though I performed it in concert, it's also a song that's often performed at weddings, funerals and religious services because it evokes feelings of peace, devotion and reverence.

We've all heard the classic proverb, 'Behind every great man, there's a great woman.' And this remark is certainly true in both J.S. Bach's and Charles Gounod's cases. Even though he was orphaned at such a young age, Bach's life was deeply influenced by the women around him. His first wife, Maria Barbara Bach, and his second wife, Anna Magdalena Bach, played significant roles in his personal and professional life. Anna Magdalena, in particular, was a talented singer and helped copy his manuscripts. And let's not forget that between them they gave birth to Bach's twenty children.

Charles Gounod's life was also shaped by the women in it. His mother, Victoire Lemachois Gounod, was a talented pianist who played a crucial role in his musical education. After his father died, when Charles was just five, she supported the family by giving piano lessons. She recognised her son's talent early and guided his studies, eventually helping him enter the Paris Conservatoire. Charles married

Anna Zimmerman, the daughter of Pierre-Joseph-Guillaume Zimmerman, a renowned pianist and professor at the Paris Conservatoire. Her family's musical background and influence also played a role in Gounod's career.

I was fortunate, unlike Bach, growing up, to have very supportive parents (my mum, it's fair to say, spoilt me rotten) and I'm so thankful that I had a strong family foundation that allowed me to go and do my thing; just knowing that I had their unending support and love helped me navigate what could have been a very tricky period. My parents gave up so much of their free time due to my heavy workload. They also carefully guided my early career, much like Gounod's mother helped him. Mum also made sure that my home life was as normal as possible, even though everything else happening around me was far from normal.

So, just like Johann Sebastian Bach and Charles Gounod, I've been very fortunate in my life to have been influenced by some amazing women. I get to work with incredible women who inspire and teach me every day. Closer to home, my mother is one of the kindest people I know, a loving parent who has always been so selfless. When I was a child chorister, she spent hours driving me to and from Bangor Cathedral. She also accompanied me, more often than not, when I made the incessant trips from North Wales down to London to appear on television and radio shows or when I

sang in concerts. (For the record, my dad also did his bit, but in this part of the book I'm concentrating on the girls!) She was even my primary school teacher from the ages of four to seven. I called her Mrs Jones at school and Mam at home, and she was tougher on me than my fellow classmates, but we made it work. As a teacher, she was sympathetic, patient, loving and fun, and was all those things as a mum also. She was the glue that kept my childhood extended family together: we'd spend weekends visiting grandparents and aunts and uncles and I consider myself so lucky to have had this carefree, idyllic upbringing.

I have also been blessed by marriage. My wife Claire is my best friend. She's also a compassionate, loving person who always puts others first. A strong, very level-headed person, she always keeps me on the straight and narrow. I tend to be more emotional, impulsive and dramatic and she manages to keep my feet on the ground. I can't thank her enough for putting up with me! She puts me right when needed, and even though I may not appreciate it at the time, she's (almost!) always right. She has been the best mother to our children, who in turn have turned into amazing young people. Lucas is a considerate and good person and I'm very proud of the young man he is. He cares deeply about people and the planet we live on. I could wax lyrical about his attributes, but, as I say, this little section is all about the girls! Emilia has a heart full of kindness, a laugh

that's contagious, and a spirit that embraces every moment with joy and enthusiasm. She brings light into every room and makes the people around her feel valued and happy. I am a very lucky man.

On the eighth and fifteenth of this month, International Women's Day and Mothering Sunday, I may well offer up a Hail Mary prayer of thanks to the heavens, and I will, most definitely, be honouring the wonderful women in my life. I am so lucky to have them in my life.

1 March: *St David's Day*

Courage cannot be counterfeited. It is one
virtue that escapes hypocrisy.

NAPOLEON BONAPARTE

2 March

Who waits until the wind shall silent keep,
Will never find the ready hour to sow.

HELEN HUNT JACKSON, 'Chance'

3 March

I have always observed that to succeed in the world one should appear like a fool but be wise.

MONTESQUIEU, *Pensées*

4 March: *Holi*

A good person dyes events with his own colour . . . and turns whatever happens to his own benefit.

SENECA

5 March

Fame is a bee,
It has a song –
It has a sting –
Ah, too, it has a wing.

EMILY DICKINSON, '1763'

6 March:
Winter Paralympics, Italy

Do your duty, and leave the rest to heaven.

PIERRE CORNEILLE, *Horace*

7 March

Joy is prayer; joy is strength: joy is love;
joy is a net of love by which you can catch souls.

MOTHER TERESA

8 March:
International Women's Day

The older one gets, the more one feels that the
present moment must be enjoyed, comparable
to a state of grace.

MARIE CURIE, *Madame Curie*

9 March

If you want to be happy, be.

LEO TOLSTOY

What simple things bring you happiness?

10 March

If you're not making mistakes, then
you're not doing anything. I'm positive
that a doer makes mistakes.

JOHN WOODEN

11 March

Trust in dreams, for in them is hidden
the gate to eternity.

KAHLIL GIBRAN, *The Prophet*

12 March

Work hard, stay positive, and get up early.
It's the best part of the day.

GEORGE ALLEN, SR

13 March

Your destiny is to fulfill those things upon which you focus most intently. So choose to keep your focus on that which is truly magnificent, beautiful, uplifting and joyful. Your life is always moving toward something.

RALPH MARSTON

14 March

When you show deep empathy toward others, their defensive energy goes down, and positive energy replaces it. That's when you can get more creative in solving problems.

STEPHEN COVEY

15 March: *Mothering Sunday*

Stay positive and happy. Work hard and don't give up hope. Be open to criticism and keep learning. Surround yourself with happy, warm and genuine people.

TENA DESAE

Is there something you'd like to learn or learn more about this spring?

16 March

Be like a postage stamp. Stick to one thing till you get there.

JOSH BILLINGS

17 March: *St Patrick's Day*

Be happy with what you have and you will have plenty to be happy about.

Irish Proverb

18 March

The secret of genius is to carry the spirit of the child into old age, which means never losing your enthusiasm.

ALDOUS HUXLEY

19 March

Your children are not your children.

They are sons and daughters of Life's longing for itself.

They come through you but not from you.

And though they are with you yet they belong not to you.

You may give them your love but not your thoughts,

For they have their own thoughts.

You may house their bodies but not their souls,

For their souls dwell in the house of tomorrow, which you cannot visit, not even in your dreams.

You may strive to be like them, but seek not to make them like you.

For life goes not backward nor tarries with yesterday.

You are the bows from which your children as living arrows are sent forth.

The archer sees the make upon the path of the infinite, and He bends you with His might that His arrows may go swift and far.

Let your bending in the archer's hand be for gladness.

For even as He loves the arrow that flies, so He also loves the bow that is stable.

KAHLIL GIBRAN, The Prophet

20 March: *Spring Equinox*

When adversity strikes, that's when you have
to be the most calm. Take a step back, stay strong,
stay grounded and press on.

LL COOL J

Is there something difficult in your life that is worth persevering with?

21 March

All things are difficult before they are easy.

THOMAS FULLER, *Gnomologia*

22 March

Nothing will work unless you do.

MAYA ANGELOU

23 March

Let us realize that: the privilege to work is a gift, the power to work is a blessing, the love of work is success!

DAVID O. MCKAY, General Conference,
Church of Jesus Christ of Latter-day Saints, October 1909

24 March

Think in the morning. Act in the noon. Eat in the evening. Sleep in the night.

WILLIAM BLAKE, *The Marriage of Heaven and Hell*

25 March

It is far better to be alone than to be in bad company.

GEORGE WASHINGTON

26 March

Work hard for what you want because it won't come to you without a fight. You have to be strong and courageous and know that you can do anything you put your mind to. If somebody puts you down or criticizes you, just keep on believing in yourself and turn it into something positive.

LEAH LABELLE

27 March

Would you have a great empire? Rule over yourself.

PUBLIUS SYRUS

28 March: *Earth Hour*

We must all either wear out or rust out, every one
of us. My choice is to wear out.

THEODORE ROOSEVELT,
'The Strenuous Life', 1899

29 March:
Palm Sunday (Clocks Go Forward)

I would always rather be happy than dignified.

CHARLOTTE BRONTË, *Jane Eyre*

30 March

The best men are not those who have waited for chances, but who have taken them; besieged chance, conquered the chance, and made chance the servitor.

E.H. CHAPIN, *Pushing to the Front*

31 March

In the meantime, cling tooth and nail to the following rule: not to give in to adversity, not to trust prosperity, and always take full note of fortune's habit of behaving just as she pleases.

SENECA, *Letters from a Stoic*

Notes for March

April

Sergei Rachmaninov –
Piano Concerto No. 2

'Music is enough for a lifetime, but a lifetime
is not enough for music.'

SERGEI RACHMANINOV

The Hall of Fame is an annual compilation of the 300 most popular classical works as polled by listeners of Classic FM through a public vote. For the last thirty years the radio station has counted down from three hundred to one, over the Easter weekend. It's the world's largest survey of classical music tastes, and for well over a decade I've been involved in announcing the chart. Every January listeners are asked to get in touch, naming their three favourite pieces of music. The information is then gathered, numbers crunched and put into a top 300 chart. It's a real privilege and an honour to be part

of something so exciting, and the listeners are often equally, if not more, excited than I am. Some hold parties where they listen together, some FaceTime family and friends so they can be together to whoop with joy and gasp in horror at the risers and fallers. Some keep files and detailed notes from previous years so that they can cross-examine. I've even had listeners say they're playing drinking games trying to guess which piece comes next!

Mozart, Rachmaninov and Vaughan Williams have been among the composers who have topped the poll in recent years. But Bruch also took the Number 1 spot for several years. And, although Beethoven always has a strong presence in the top 300, he's never taken that coveted top spot. Since 2013, soundtracks for video games like *Final Fantasy*, *Banjo-Kazooie* and *The Elder Scrolls* have been climbing up the chart, while film maestro John Williams took the crown as the most popular living composer in 2023, which also saw a record number of movie scores in the top 300. The Easter weekend countdown is a big thing, with millions getting involved and listening all over the world. It reinforces the fact that classical music is universally loved and has the power to move people emotionally, mentally and physically.

I have known this to be true ever since I was a seven-year-old child. One of the first pieces of classical music I heard and took in was Rachmaninov's *Piano Concerto No. 2*. I had no idea what it was or who wrote it at the time. I woke up in my bed at our house in North Wales to this beautiful music coming from my parents' radio and filling every room, with the smell of bacon filling my nostrils as my mother prepared Sunday breakfast. I jumped out of bed, eager not to miss the announcer giving the details of the piece. And that was it: my love affair with classical music had begun.

Saturday afternoons were spent either in WH Smith's or Woolworth's deliberating over what cassette or vinyl to buy with my meagre wage packet from Bangor Cathedral. It wasn't long until I had my very own copy of the Rachmaninov classic, and as a bonus the album also had his gorgeous 'Vocalise' piece, along with his 'Rhapsody on a Theme of Paganini'. I was in seventh heaven! I played that record repeatedly and the rapturous slow second movement became my 'go-to' in life's more emotional moments. His lush harmonies, sweeping melodies and emotional depth capture the essence of longing, devotion and heartache.

But's not just me who turns to this music in times of need, be that death, birth, love or break-up. Rachmaninov's *Piano Concerto No. 2* of 1901 is often described as the greatest piano concerto ever written and when Classic FM combined the positions of the first fifteen years of its annual Hall of Fame chart, the work came out on top overall as the nation's favourite classical work. It topped the chart in 2024 too. It seems the nation just can't get enough of it.

It's incredible to think that it almost didn't get written. When Rachmaninov started composing this towering piano masterpiece in 1900, he was in a terrible emotional state after having been absolutely pilloried in the press for his Symphony No. 1 a couple of years earlier. His confidence was shot, and he was riddled with self-doubt. Thankfully, though, Rachmaninov had a good therapist who came to the rescue. His name was Nikolai Dahl and quite rightly the concerto is dedicated to him.

Rachmaninov later recalled, 'I heard the same hypnotic formula repeated day after day while I lay half asleep in the armchair in Dahl's study. "You will write a Concerto . . . You will work with great facility . . . It will be excellent". And it worked! The second piano concerto was Rachmaninov's comeback, and it was a huge commercial smash – just what he needed.

The second movement of the concerto is pure unadulterated sentimentality, forever associated too with the 1945 black-and-white romantic film *Brief Encounter*. The director David Lean chose to employ the piano concerto to capture the emotion felt, but not fully expressed, by star-crossed lovers Celia Johnson and Trevor Howard. For many filmgoers it was the introduction to Rachmaninov's music and the music, in return, has become inextricably linked to the movie. The whistle of a steam train whooshing through the station ushers in the tune and the turbulent mood is set . . . Now I really want to watch the movie again!

That main melody is so good that American songwriter Eric Carmen nabbed it for his song 'All By Myself', later covered famously by Celine Dion. It was a worldwide hit for her, selling millions of copies. It was later used to great effect in the movie *Bridget Jones's Diary*. In the iconic scene which I love so much, Bridget, played by Renée Zellweger, sits alone in her pyjamas, drinking wine and singing along to Celine Dion's version of the song. The moment perfectly encapsulates loneliness, self-pity and humour. The music and the scene are just so relatable – a wry symbol of single life and a hope for love. And such is the power of Rachmaninov's tune that it was also used in my favourite television series *Friends*. Who can forget Chandler's depression after Joey moved out of their flat!

I think Rachmaninov was so right when he said: 'Music is enough for a lifetime, but a lifetime is not enough for music.' Because music is vast, spanning cultures, genres and emotions. You can dedicate your whole life to studying, composing or, in my case, performing music, yet still there will always be more to discover. Music evolves continuously. Its emotional and intellectual impact deepens over time, revealing new meanings with each experience. While one lifetime allows immersion in music's richness, it is not enough to grasp its entirety. I am so happy, though, that I have had a lifetime to enjoy Rachmaninov's piece. It's filled with rich harmonies that swell like waves of emotion, mirroring the highs and lows of life itself. Whether through his personal experiences or his innate ability to capture human emotion, Rachmaninov's music remains one of the most profound expressions of love in classical music history.

So maybe this month, if you're in a relationship, forgo buying the red roses and instead get your loved one a copy of Rachmaninov's *Piano Concerto No. 2*. But if, as Celine would sing, you're 'all by yourself', and you 'don't want to be', then pour yourself something nice, play the record, crank the volume up to max and let this gorgeous music be enough.

1 April: *Passover*

To share your weakness is to make yourself vulnerable;
to make yourself vulnerable is to show your strength.

CRISS JAMI, *Killosophy*

2 April

Suffering has been stronger than all other teaching,
and has taught me to understand what your heart used
to be. I have been bent and broken, but – I hope – into
a better shape.

CHARLES DICKENS, *Great Expectations*

3 April: *Good Friday (Bank Holiday)*

The weaker you are the louder you bark.

MASASHI KISHIMOTO, *Impassioned Efforts*

4 April

For the first time in my life I began to realise that it is not evil and brutality, but nearly always weakness, that is to blame for the worst things that happen in this world.

STEFAN ZWEIG, *Beware of Pity*

5 April: *Easter Sunday*

Do not abandon yourselves to despair.
We are the Easter people and hallelujah is our song.

POPE JOHN PAUL II, 30 November 1986

6 April: *Easter Monday (Bank Holiday)*

The secret of happiness is freedom and the secret of freedom is courage.

THUCYDIDES, History of the Peloponnesian War

7 April

It does not matter how slowly you go as long as you do not stop.

CONFUCIUS

8 April

Something of greater import, I think, is to say I'm blessed in infinitely many ways. But sometimes I just don't see it.

BONIFACE SAGINI, *Thrills and Chills*

This Easter season, where would you like to see despair replaced with hope?

9 April

Regardless of what is going on in your life, no matter how hurtful, and dark things seem, hold on to optimism. Wonder what wonderful thing will happen to you today? Leave your heart open to blessings, and spread your sunshine to others. They could be feeling down, and the sunshine that surrounds you could lift them up? In reflection, the kindness you share will always return your way. God bless.

RON BARATONO

10 April

One single grateful thought raised to heaven is the most perfect prayer.

GOTTHOLD EPHRAIM LESSING,
The Soldier's Happiness

11 April

Correction does much, but encouragement does more.

JOHANN WOLFGANG VON GOETHE,
Letter to A.F. Oeser, 9 November 1768

12 April

When push comes to shove, it ain't the science that's going to lift you up – it's the belief, the spiritual side of life, that's going to lift you up, no matter what religion you are.

KIRSTIE ALLEY

13 April

I believe if you keep your faith, you keep your trust, you keep the right attitude, if you're grateful, you'll see God open up new doors.

JOEL OSTEEN

14 April

Guilt is just as powerful, but its influence is positive, while shame's is destructive. Shame erodes our courage and fuels disengagement.

BRENÉ BROWN, *Daring Greatly*

15 April

When you look at people who are successful, you will find that they aren't the people who are motivated, but have consistency in their motivation.

ARSENE WENGER

Take a moment to ponder how you are blessed today.

16 April

Your living is determined not so much
by what life brings to you as by the attitude
you bring to life; not so much by what
happens to you as by the way your mind
looks at what happens.

KAHLIL GIBRAN

17 April

Success is dependent on effort.

SOPHOCLES

18 April

I know you've heard it a thousand times before. But it's true – hard work pays off. If you want to be good, you have to practice, practice, practice. If you don't love something, then don't do it.

RAY BRADBURY, *Ray Bradbury Uncensored!*

19 April

Never limit your view of life by any past experience.

ERNEST HOLMES, *The Science of Mind*

20 April

What is rightly done, however humble, is noble.

SIR HENRY ROYCE

21 April

The human frame being what it is, heart, body and brain all mixed together, and not contained in separate compartments as they will be no doubt in another million years, a good dinner is of great importance to good talk. One cannot think well, love well, sleep well, if one has not dined well.

VIRGINIA WOOLF, *A Room of One's Own*

22 April

An eye for an eye only ends up making the whole world blind.

MAHATMA GANDI

23 April: *St George's Day*

If we believe that tomorrow will be better, we can bear a hardship today.

THICH NHAT HANH, *Peace Is Every Step*

What are the things you know that you have to 'keep going' with?

24 April

If I had to name my greatest strength, I guess it would be my humility. Greatest weakness, it's possible that I'm a little too awesome.

BARACK OBAMA, New York, 2008

25 April

I hope you realize that every day is a fresh start for you. That every sunrise is a new chapter in your life waiting to be written.

JUANSEN DIZON, *Confessions of a Wallflower*

26 April

Forgiveness says you are given another chance
to make a new beginning.

DESMOND TUTU

27 April

Stay away from what might have been, and look at what can be.

MARSHA PETRIE SUE

28 April

Have the courage to follow your heart and intuition.
They somehow know what you truly want to become.

STEVE JOBS,
Stanford University commencement speech, 2005

29 April

Under the comb, the tangle and the straight path are
the same.

HERACLITUS

30 April

Stop being afraid of what could go wrong, and start being excited about what could go right.

TONY ROBBINS

Notes for April

May

Gabriel Fauré – 'Pie Jesu'

'Soul and spirit guide the game.'

ROGER FEDERER

On the stage, I hit high notes. On the court, I hit winners! Each year, I can't wait for the tennis season to begin and I'm full of anticipation during the month of May.

Ever since I was young, I've wanted to win Wimbledon. As soon as the evenings became longer and the sunshine started appearing in May, we'd line up the metal bins in the school yard to act as the net and play for hours, until it got too dark to see the ball. I had the John McEnroe Dunlop Maxply wooden racket; I even had the sweatband! If there was a dubious line call, then we'd deliver the obligatory McEnroe rant 'You cannot be serious!!' in a very bad American accent.

Tennis was my second favourite sport to play, after football. I have always had good hand–eye coordination, so found hitting the tennis ball quite easy. I continued to play throughout my childhood and took it to another level when I joined Bangor Tennis Club in my late teens. Out went the wooden racket, to be replaced by a snazzy carbon fibre one. That's when tennis became serious. I played for hours on end when my voice started to change, sometimes up to five hours a day. It's fair to say that tennis filled the hole that not being able to sing left behind. One triumph from this time was that my partner and I won the North Wales Schools Mixed Doubles Competition. Little did I know that my tennis 'claim to fame' had only just begun.

Through my singing, I had been invited by the Lawn Tennis Association to attend a few tennis events in London and had even frequented Wimbledon quite a few times. I was there when Pat Cash beat Ivan Lendl in the Wimbledon final. As a die-hard Lendl fan, who copied the tennis great by also having sawdust in my pocket to mop up hand sweat, I was devastated when he lost in the final. I was in the posh posh seats and was told off for not standing up and giving Pat Cash an ovation!

I was eighteen years old and so excited when the invitation came for me to present the Wightman Cup

weekend from the Royal Albert Hall in London – a venue I'd sung in many times as a boy but had no idea that it also hosted a tennis tournament between the American and British Ladies. My job was just to introduce the players, and I couldn't be happier, especially when I found out that the US were sending their best stars to compete. The Royal Albert Hall is certainly one of my favourite halls in the world to sing in, and I must admit to also loving it as a tennis venue. The seats on ground level are replaced by just one court, and it looks resplendent as the centre of focus, instead of the usual stage.

I had been asked to turn up early on the Sunday morning and to bring my tennis racket and kit. I had no idea what had been planned, but when I walked into the auditorium, I was met by the American and number 4 ranked player in the world, Zina Garrison. She'd heard I could play a bit and was there to challenge me to a game! I was a quivering wreck as I faced one of the world's best players at the other end of the court. Her first serve was an ace: I didn't even have time to swing my racket back for the return. Less than half-an-hour later she'd thrashed me. On some points, she even told me where she was going to hit the ball, and I still couldn't return it! I won only a handful of points, but it was an experience I'll never forget. I got to talk to her about her life on the tennis circuit and she, in turn, asked me about life as a singer. What happened next has become the stuff of legend within my circle of friends. Back in the late 1960s the Royal Albert Hall echo became a thing of the past when large fibreglass acoustic diffusing discs were installed, commonly known as 'mushrooms'. At the end of our match, Zina and I tried knocking tennis balls into the mushrooms high above us and then retired to the changing rooms, still laughing at our foolish endeavours.

Spool forward twenty-odd years and I was about to walk onto stage at the Royal Albert Hall to present a special concert, when one of the management team came up to me and, in front of the whole crew gathered, said that they'd recently lowered the mushrooms for cleaning and had found two tennis balls in one of them. Those balls had probably interfered with the hall's acoustic for years, ruining concerts for hundreds of thousands of audience members. I went bright red with embarrassment and then everyone fell about laughing. It was a perfect set up! They had indeed found two tennis balls in a 'mushroom', but the sound had not been affected, thankfully. They also found a pair of false teeth in the disc (I promise that the teeth had nothing to do with me or Zina!).

I was only eleven when I first appeared on the Royal Albert Hall stage and one of the pieces I sang was Gabriel Fauré's 'Pie Jesu'. It's part of the composer's *Requiem*, and is a firm favourite with young choristers. Unlike some other composers' requiems (remember Mozart's we looked at in January?), Fauré's is serene and comforting rather than dramatic and turbulent. It's a magical piece that offers enduring peace and rest. For me, the 'Pie Jesu' is a real highlight, with its ethereal quality, and a flowing, chant-like melody. It conveys a sense of deep solace and spirituality, reflecting Fauré's unique approach to sacred music. I also found it to be very difficult to sing well: the phrases are long and sustained and one can easily run out of breath. Furthermore, because the voice is so exposed under the simple accompanying chords, the tuning must be bang on and many boys struggle to keep in tune throughout. But the 'Pie Jesu' always sounded special in the vast arena of the Royal Albert Hall.

Gabriel Urbain Fauré was born in 1845 and, as far as I'm concerned, is one of the most influential French composers, making a massive contribution to modern French music. I love his refined harmonies and lyrical melodies. Whenever I sang 'Pie Jesu' in concert, whether in a sacred setting or in the Royal Albert Hall, I felt a real connection with my higher power, and also breathed a huge sigh of relief, and thanked God, if I managed to get to the end without a glitch.

Fauré's family, like mine, had no significant musical background. His dad was a teacher and his mum was from an aristocratic background. The youngest of six children, he always displayed musical talent and, like me, was immersed in church music from a very young age. Unlike me, he was taught by the legendary French composer Camille Saint-Saëns! Fauré was at home writing sacred and secular music; he was an influential figure in Parisian musical society and became director of the Paris Conservatoire of Music. He was also an important composer for me as a boy and continues to be to this day.

One of the highlights of my teenage years was when the then Wimbledon referee, the lovely Alan Mills, invited me to Wimbledon to have a game with him. He was a fan of my music and as a real treat we got to play on one of the main courts. After getting changed in the men's locker room, which was so thrilling, I was so pumped up for the match and thought Alan, who was more seasoned in age, was going to be a walkover. How wrong I was! I should have done my research, because he was a former Davis Cup captain and certainly knew his way around the court.

I loved that morning at the All England Club and I was so thankful to Alan. My tennis, though, had been abysmal. I was walking in the air when I stepped onto the court, but by the end of the match, I walked off in desp-air! To be fair, grass was not my natural habitat; clay was my surface of choice, and I reckon I might have fared better had our match taken place at the home of the French Open, Roland Garros, in Paris. That championship, which takes place as a precursor to Wimbledon, on 24 May, was founded back in 1925, a year after my favourite French composer Fauré died. The Parisian Championship was also a favourite of the legendary tennis player Rafael Nadal who holds the record for the most French Open men's singles titles, with fourteen victories. He's quoted as once saying: 'Play with heart, play with soul', which I think is also a very apt quote when it comes to singing Gabriel Fauré's music, especially his 'Pie Jesu'. You must sing with heart and sing with soul to serve up a winning performance.

1 May: *May Day*

My motivation is tomorrow, just one day
at a time, right?

RAFAEL NADAL

2 May

If you must have motivation, think of your paycheck on Friday.

NOEL COWARD

3 May

My attitude is that if you push me towards something that you think is a weakness, then I will turn that perceived weakness into a strength.

MICHAEL JORDAN

4 May: *Bank Holiday*

Everybody is equally weak on the inside, just that some
present their ruins as new castles and become kings.

SIMONA PANOVA, *Nightmarish Sacrifice*

5 May

You are only as invincible as your smallest weakness,
and those are tiny indeed – the length of a sleeping baby's
eyelash, the span of a child's hand. Life turns on a dime,
and – it turns out – so does one's conscience.

JODI PICOULT, *Perfect Match*

6 May

Giants are not what we think they are. The same qualities that appear to give them strength are often the sources of great weakness.

MALCOLM GLADWELL, David and Goliath

7 May

Trust yourself. You know more than you think you do.

BENJAMIN SPOCK, *Baby and Child Care*

8 May

While you are going through your trial, you can recall your past victories and count the blessings that you do have with a sure hope of greater ones to allow if you are faithful.

EZRA TAFT BENSON,
The Teachings of Ezra Benson

What are your victories so far in life?

9 May

An arrogant person considers himself perfect. This is the chief harm of arrogance. It interferes with a person's main task in life – becoming a better person.

LEO TOLSTOY, *A Calendar of Wisdom*

10 May

Few things in the world are more powerful than a positive push. A smile. A world of optimism and hope. A 'you can do it' when things are tough.

RICHARD M. DEVOS

11 May

Pessimism leads to weakness, optimism to power.

WILLIAM JAMES,
The Varieties of Religious Experience

12 May

Winners make a habit of manufacturing their own positive expectations in advance of the event.

BRIAN TRACY

13 May

Do your duty quietly and cheerfully

JOHANN WOLFGANG VON GOETHE,
Maxims and Reflections

14 May

Don't forget to tell yourself positive things daily!
You must love yourself internally to glow externally.

HANNAH BRONFMAN

What positive things could you tell
yourself today?

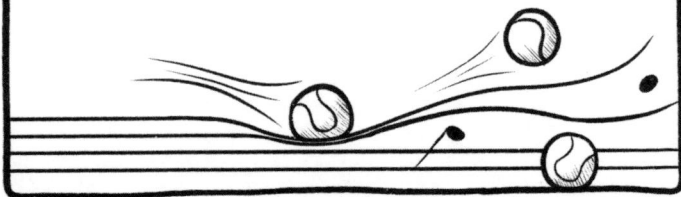

15 May

Perpetual optimism is a force multiplier.

COLIN POWELL

16 May

Desire is the key to motivation, but it's determination and commitment to an unrelenting pursuit of your goal – a commitment to excellence – that will enable you to attain the success you seek.

MARIO ANDRETTI

17 May

The greatest discovery of my generation is that a human being can alter his life by altering his attitude.

WILLIAM JAMES,
The Will to Believe and Other Essays in Popular Philosophy

In this season of new beginnings, is there something you feel ready to release control over?

18 May

Calm mind brings inner strength and self-confidence, so that's very important for good health.

DALAI LAMA

19 May

Luck is a dividend of sweat. The more you sweat, the luckier you get.

RAY KROC

20 May

Believe you can and you're halfway there.

THEODORE ROOSEVELT

21 May

Don't let the force of an impression when it first hits you knock you off your feet; just say to it, 'Hold on a moment; let me see who you are and what you represent. Let me put you to the test.'

EPICTETUS, *Discourses*

22 May

Genius is the ability to put into effect what is in the mind. There's no other definition of it.

F. SCOTT FITZGERALD, *The Crack-Up*

23 May

Wise men are able to make a fitting use even
of their enmities.

PLUTARCH, *Moralia*

24 May: *French Open Tennis / Pentecost*

Everybody wants to go to heaven, but nobody wants to die.

JOE LEWIS

25 May: *Bank Holiday*

If you die in an elevator, be sure to push the Up button.

SAM LEVENSON,
You Don't Have To Be In Who's Who To Know What's What

26 May

A journey of a thousand miles begins with a single step.

LAO TZU, *Tao Te Ching*

27 May

I will be calm. I will be mistress of myself.

JANE AUSTEN, *Sense and Sensibility*

28 May

Isn't it nice to think that tomorrow is a new day
with no mistakes in it yet?

L.M. MONTGOMERY, *Anne of Green Gables*

29 May

Be willing to be a beginner every single morning.

MEISTER ECKHART

30 May

Do not wait until the conditions are perfect to begin. Beginning makes the conditions perfect.

ALAN COHEN

31 May

And now here is my secret, a very simple secret: It is only with the heart that one can see rightly; what is essential is invisible to the eye.

ANTOINE DE SAINT-EXUPÉRY, *The Little Prince*

Notes for May

June

Edward Elgar – 'Pomp and Circumstance', March No.1 in D Major

'The music is in the air. Take as much as you want.'

EDWARD ELGAR

During the month of June, traditionally the start of British outdoor summer concerts season, it's not just music that's in the air – it's rain. Sometimes torrential rain. Sometimes apocalyptic downpours on a biblical scale. But nearly always . . . rain!

We 'take it' here in the UK because we have no choice. I can't tell you how many open-air prom concerts I've performed in that have been a total wash-out. I've seen first hand how these events can make or break the poor concert promoter. It was W.C. Fields who remarked, 'If at first you don't succeed, try, try again. Then quit. There's no point in being a damn fool about it.' The British concert promoter is a hardy soul, it seems, and ever the optimist. It's not a vocation for the faint hearted. When the concert promoter books the date and the outdoor venue, which, in many cases, is basically a very large field, they must do so while offering a prayer up to God for fine weather. It's a total lottery!

On a very rare fine day, when the sun is shining, the occasion can be resplendent and utterly thrilling. Picture the scene: 20,000 people in a field somewhere in England's green and pleasant land, a sea of flags being waved to the beat, as a conductor, in his smart, black dinner jacket whips up a hundred-piece orchestra to perform Elgar's 'Land of Hope and Glory'. At an opportune moment, all eyes are trained towards heaven as a Spitfire flies overhead. It swells the heart and stirs the soul! I've been very fortunate to present and sing at hundreds of these events across the country over the decades and I love them, come rain or shine. And this is the surprising bit: rain doesn't usually dampen any spirits. I'm always amazed by how 'up for it' the crowd is, even if they are soaking wet and cold!

Maybe it's the music being performed that plays a big part in keeping the audience buoyant. If that is the case, then a huge 'thank you' should go to English composer Edward Elgar. His music is at the heart of summer prom season, which is rather fitting as he was born on 2 June 1857. It's fitting too because Elgar loved the countryside, particularly the Malvern Hills, where he often found inspiration for his music. He also enjoyed cycling, and even though he was a rather complex character who struggled with self-doubt and insecurity, I'm sure he and I would have got on, if only because he gave whimsical names to his bicycles! His most famous bicycle was named Mr Phoebus. I remember finding this out as a child at school and immediately deciding that my beloved bike also needed a name. Looking back, I'm rather embarrassed that all I came up with was Brian! Elgar's superior bike name likely comes from Phoebus Apollo, the Greek and Roman god of the sun, light and music. Given Elgar's love for cycling and nature, he may have chosen the name as a playful and poetic reference to his bike as a source of freedom and inspiration – just as Apollo was associated with enlightenment and creativity. All in all, he chose a perfect name for his bike, even if the god of sun lets us down quite a lot!

So, cycling became a cherished part of Elgar's routine much as his music has become a cherished part of our summer, whatever the weather. I relish performing at these concerts so I hope they will continue to be put on. They make me proud to be British; I love the fact that thousands of people descend on a muddy field with picnic hampers and deckchairs, and even in the face of adversity, display such stoicism and determination to have a good time.

It was raining so heavily once at a concert I presented in Hampton Court, that when I walked onto stage all I could see were thousands of multicoloured ponchos covering every inch of the bodies assembled, but for their eyes. It was a very spooky, unnerving experience. On that occasion the audience didn't even clap for fear of getting drenched. But everyone gave a standing ovation at the end of the concert (it was either an ovation or people couldn't wait to get up and get dry!)

Closer to home, I was for many years a guest at my friend and fellow Welshman and singer Bryn Terfel's Faenol Festival. I remember presenting the classical evening, which was always the night before the headline act's performance; and this particular year Van Morrison was going to be closing the festival. It was a bleak, cold, rainy evening and many thousands of music fans had turned up to enjoy Bryn, myself and the orchestra, who of course would be performing some Elgar! As I stood on stage mid-song, I noticed a very bright light trying to knife through the storm, and as it got closer, the noise got louder and louder; a deep 'whomp-whomp-whomp' sound. I honestly thought the aliens were descending and even the orchestra stopped playing. Eventually we all realised that it was Van Morrison's helicopter trying its hardest to land through the relentless drumming of the rain. I've never seen anyone as happy as Van was, eventually having his feet on solid ground!

I also once did an open-air prom concert in the grounds of Chatsworth House in front of 40,000 very soggy concertgoers. Rain did not stop play that evening either. I was amazed by the efforts people had gone to to make the afternoon special. Some had such elaborate set-ups with tables, white tablecloths and candelabras, and even the finest bone china and crystal-cut champagne flutes. I'm not exaggerating when I say that I once witnessed a family arrive for a concert with their own portable toilet!

We are a nation that always tries to make the best of it, hoping for triumph over adversity. That's why Edward Elgar's music fits so well. It stirs the soul because it blends deep emotion with grandeur, creating a profound sense of nostalgia, triumph and longing. His melodies, rich with lyrical beauty, evoke both personal reflection and pride. And this 'never say die' attitude will be very evident this month as Canada, Mexico and the US host the twenty-third FIFA World Cup, the quadrennial international men's football championship. Ever since I was a very young boy, I've always been captivated by the competition. During the World Cup, an electrifying atmosphere sweeps across countries, uniting people of all backgrounds. Streets, homes and public squares burst with colour as fans proudly display their national flags. Strangers become friends, sharing the excitement. It's just like a summer prom concert in a way. It fosters a rare sense of unity and galvanises people.

Ever the optimist, I am of course cheering on Wales, if they make it into the competition. Our track record isn't great, only qualifying for two tournaments in 1958 and 2022.

But that doesn't stop me dreaming of the big win. And to paraphrase one of Elgar's most stirring pieces, history might dictate that we're the land of no glory when it comes to the biggest competitions but there's always hope. There is *always* hope, even in the pouring rain.

1 June

You've done it before and you can do it now. See the positive possibilities. Redirect the substantial energy of your frustration and turn it into positive, effective, unstoppable determination.

RALPH MARSTON

2 June

Weak people believe what is forced on them. Strong people what they wish to believe, forcing that to be real.

GENE WOLFE, *Shadow & Claw*

3 June

A fear of weakness only strengthens weakness.

CRISS JAMI, Salomé

4 June

I'd rather sing one wild song and burst my heart
with it, than live a thousand years watching my
digestion and being afraid of the wet.

JACK LONDON, The Turtles of Tasman

5 June

Most folks are as happy as they make up their minds to be.

ABRAHAM LINCOLN

6 June

Your success and happiness lies in you. Resolve to keep happy, and your joy and you shall form an invincible host against difficulties.

HELEN KELLER, *Out of the Dark*

7 June

I always like to look on the optimistic side of
life, but I am realistic enough to know that life is
a complex matter.

WALT DISNEY

8 June

Positive anything is better than negative nothing.

ELBERT HUBBARD

What three positive things can you remember
at the start of this week?

9 June

The best thing to do when you find yourself in a hurting or vulnerable place is to surround yourself with the strongest, finest, most positive people you know.

KRISTIN ARMSTRONG

10 June: *100th Anniversary of Gaudi's Death*

Positive thinking is more than just a tagline. It changes the way we behave. And I firmly believe that when I am positive, it not only makes me better, but it also makes those around me better.

HARVEY MACKAY,
'Avoid Bad Habits of Self-Defeating People'

11 June:
FIFA Football World Cup, Canada, Mexico and US

Resilience isn't a single skill. It's a variety of skills and coping mechanisms. To bounce back from bumps in the road as well as failures, you should focus on emphasizing the positive.

JEAN CHATZKY

12 June

Belief is a wise wager. Granted that faith cannot be proved, what harm will come to you if you gamble on its truth and it proves false? If you gain, you gain all; if you lose, you lose nothing. Wager, then, without hesitation, that He exists.

BLAISE PASCAL, *Pensées*

13 June: *Trooping the Colour*

It's really a wonder that I haven't dropped all my ideals, because they seem so absurd and impossible to carry out. Yet I keep them, because in spite of everything I still believe that people are really good at heart.

ANNE FRANK, *The Diary of a Young Girl*

14 June

You cannot control what happens to you, but you can control your attitude toward what happens to you, and in that, you will be mastering change rather than allowing it to master you.

BRIAN TRACY

15 June

A positive attitude causes a chain reaction of positive thoughts, events and outcomes. It is a catalyst and it sparks extraordinary results.

WADE BOGGS

16 June

Serenity is knowing that your worst shot is still pretty good.

JOHNNY MILLER

17 June

Remain calm, serene, always in command of yourself.
You will then find out how easy it is to get along.

PARAMAHANSA YOGANANDA

What things help calm you?

18 June

All life demands struggle. Those who have everything given to them become lazy, selfish, and insensitive to the real values of life. The very striving and hard work that we so constantly try to avoid is the major building block in the person we are today.

POPE PAUL VI

19 June

The only thing that overcomes hard luck is hard work.

HARRY GOLDEN

20 June

Nature does not require that we be perfect;
it requires only that we grow, and we can do this
as well from a mistake as from a success.

JOSHUA L. LIEBMAN

21 June

Give us back our suffering, we cry to Heaven in our hearts – suffering rather than indifferentism; for out of nothing comes nothing. But out of suffering may come the cure. Better have pain than paralysis! A hundred struggle and drown in the breakers. One discovers the new world. But rather, ten times rather, die in the surf, heralding the way to that new world, than stand idly on the shore!

FLORENCE NIGHTINGALE, *Cassandra*

What could you do this week that would help others?

22 June

The human being who lives only for himself finally reaps nothing but unhappiness.

B.C. FORBES

23 June

Choose not to be harmed and you won't feel harmed. Don't feel harmed and you haven't been.

MARCUS AURELIUS, *Meditations*

24 June

What such a man needs is not courage, but nerve control, cool headedness. This he can get only by practice.

THEODORE ROOSEVELT, *An Autobiography*

25 June

Happy men and women seek nothing and do not notify others of their happiness; the unhappy are interesting, the happy are unknown.

EMILIE DU CHÂTELET, 'Discourse on Happiness'

26 June

He says the best way out is always through.
And I agree to that, or in so far
As I can see no way out, but through.

ROBERT FROST, 'A Servant to Servants'

27 June

When jarred, unavoidably, by circumstance, revert at once to yourself, and don't lose the rhythm more than you can help. You'll have a better grasp of harmony if you keep going back to it.

MARCUS AURELIUS, *Meditations*

28 June

My formula for greatness in a human being is amor fati: that one wants nothing to be different, not forward, not backward, not in all eternity. Not merely bear what is necessary, still less conceal it . . . But love it.

FRIEDRICH NIETZSCHE, *Ecce Homo*

29 June:
Wimbledon Tennis Championships

Death is nothing, but to live defeated and inglorious
is to die daily.

NAPOLEON BONAPARTE,
Letter to Jacques Lauriston, 12 December 1804

30 June

Some people are so afraid to die that they never
begin to live.

HENRY VAN DYKE

Notes for June

July

John Ireland – 'Sea Fever'

I must go down to the seas again, to the lonely sea
and the sky,
And all I ask is a tall ship and a star to steer her by,
And the wheel's kick and the wind's song and the
white sail's shaking,
And a grey mist on the sea's face and a grey dawn
breaking.

JOHN MASEFIELD

Isn't it funny how some of the things you hated as a child
give you so much pleasure as an adult? I'm not talking
about eating spinach (although I can't remember when that
vegetable went from zero to hero!).

When I was very young, I was quite nervous about the sea,
which is not ideal when you live on an island and your dad has

a sailboat. At that age the thought of spending the weekend on dad's boat, sailing and fishing, filled me with dread. I wanted instead to be playing football with my friends. I wanted to be on dry land. On the many weekends we'd be at the sea, once on board, I'd spend most of the time below deck listening to my cassettes, and while the boat shifted aggressively from left to right and up and down, I'd be singing along heartedly, a slightly nauseous feeling never far away!

But something changed as I approached my teens. I'm not aware of how or when it happened, but all of a sudden, I couldn't wait to spend July weekends out on the boat. I loved fishing, and the thrill of catching a huge dogfish; I also loved the sailing and even the cold-water swimming (yes, the sea is cold in July in North Wales!). Sometimes we'd even spend the night on the boat and, whereas this had been very much a chore and a hassle when I was child, in my adolescence it was an adventure. We'd anchor either in an idyllic spot called Abermenai, near Caernarfon, where very often we were the only ones there, or we'd sail further away from home and end up in Porthdinllaen, near Pwllheli, with amazing views across the Irish Sea and a sandy beach on its doorstep. This was home to Ty Coch, Welsh for Red House, a traditional tavern with oodles of character and a roaring real fire. Back then, everyone in that pub looked like extras from the *Pirates of the Caribbean*! It was there I tasted my first drop of real ale and

opened my first pack of salt-and-shake crisps (the concept of salting my own crisps with my very own blue sachet of salt blew my mind!). Looking back now, I miss those carefree days of summer – the busy days that would eventually give way to peaceful nights when the hypnotic effect of the sea and the distant cries of the gulls dancing on the wind would lull you into the best, deep sleep. Life was simple and wonderful: catching mackerel and cooking them moments later; not an iPhone or a computer game in sight. Instead, I had music. All kinds of music. It punctuated all aspects of my life and I was constantly surrounded by song.

Two songs were on repeat in those days. They were my highlights on a cassette called *These You Have Loved*, a collection of arias curated by the broadcaster Richard Baker. The first favourite was 'The Queen of the Night' aria from Mozart's *Magic Flute* opera. This was brilliantly sung by the great soprano Joan Sutherland (someone I would later in life work with and get to know). I would sing along with her, trying to emulate her vocal gymnastics. The other much-loved song was the aptly titled 'Sea Fever' composed by John Ireland, with words by the poet John Masefield. Ireland's music is intensely personal in style and this particular song suited me down to the ground and I would belt it out in a private performance for mum, dad and the birds and fishes of air and sea. I particularly loved the last verse and the perfect marriage of words and

music, which allowed me the opportunity to up the drama. One minute spitting words like 'whetted knife' out, the next moment shifting the dynamics on 'the long trick's over' and fading beautifully to silence. It was stunning word painting to music.

> 'I must go down to the seas again, to the vagrant
>   gypsy life,
> To the gull's way and the whale's way where the wind's
>   like a whetted knife;
> And all I ask is a merry tale from a laughing fellow-
>   rover,
> And quiet sleep and a sweet dream when the long
>   trick's over.'

John Ireland was born in Manchester and studied and taught at the Royal College of Music in London. I knew a bit about him because I adored to sing one of his hymns called 'My Song is Love Unknown' as a chorister in Bangor Cathedral. I knew even as a child how much his music resonated with me. What I didn't know back then was that his most famous song would remain with me for ever.

When I was eighteen, I became a student at the Royal Academy of Music, a prestigious musical conservatoire in London. To be fair, I was too young to be there as a student singer, because my voice had only started to change from boy to man when I was fifteen. All my contemporaries, who were much older than I was, were so intent on belting out the big arias and being opera stars that they forgot all about the more unassuming songs. But because my voice wasn't mature enough to sing opera, my singing teacher at the time – the renowned Welsh tenor Kenneth Bowen – suggested I stick to singing German Lieder, Italian Arie Antiche and English song. These are basically lyrical songs that don't require a mammoth voice to sing. Quite the opposite: it's all about putting lightness of touch and personality into the music.

My teacher introduced me to a treasure trove of lyrical pieces that were easy for me, with my very young adult voice, to sing. (It was another world-famous Welsh tenor – Stuart Burrows – who pointed out to me that my adult voice wouldn't be mature until I was in my forties. I remember my jaw hitting the floor with astonishment and fear when he gave me that bit of advice – forty seemed a million miles away and so old!) So, as a fresh-faced eighteen-year-old I decided to stick to the small stuff, and I loved every minute.

I had already enjoyed singing many of the German composer Schubert's songs as a child – songs about a happy trout darting about in the water or a little rosebush heaping revenge on an exuberant youth who snaps its branch. Equally, I adored singing songs from Arie Antiche, which was a volume of Italian antique pieces from a bygone age, and working on English songs by composers John Ireland, Roger Quilter and Benjamin Britten filled my days at college. I so enjoyed the storytelling aspect of these modest songs.

My accompanist and I would try to create a magical scene in three-and-a-half minutes of music – just one piano and one voice working together, providing the light and shade. I couldn't be happier. Yes, the songs were simple, but they were also so rewarding.

Being in London, away from home, I'd often find myself thinking of those heady days of summer on the boat with mum and dad, and as my end of first-year exam loomed closer, I had to learn a song to sing in front of a panel of experts. I decided to revisit a song from my youth: I would sing 'Sea Fever' by John Ireland. Even though the song was by now part of my DNA, I admit I was rather nervous performing it in an empty hall in front of the panel of experts. Two weeks after the exam, my singing teacher handed me an envelope with my grade and adjudication notes, which I opened with an equal measure of excitement and trepidation. What if I'd failed? What if they hated my performance? Had one of my favourite songs let me down? I needn't have worried; I was the only singer in the first year to receive an A grade. My heart was racing. Underneath my grade were typed two lines only, written by one of the examiners, who happened to be a professional singer I so admired: 'His musical brain knows exactly what to do with the music, but at the moment his young voice can't do what his brain is telling it to do!'

I smiled at my teacher, who, in return gave me a knowing look. There was the proof I needed that I was most definitely ploughing the right furrow singing my precious little songs.

The world of opera and the flashy stuff would have to wait a few more years.

That July and the early summer holiday was spent in London. The exams were done and thankfully I'd done well, so it was time to celebrate. My friends and I explored every mile of the city, burning the candle at both ends. And while it was such fun experiencing the 'hurly burly' of city life, part of me wanted to be back in North Wales, to go 'to the seas again', on the boat with mum and dad.

1 July

One of the ways to develop patience is to contemplate how patient God has been with you. When you were in times of denial, or self-abuse, or self-absorption, or hatred, God was infinitely patient. God does not scold or punish you when you are off the sacred path, nor does God desert you. This is the same kind of patience that you want to develop.

WAYNE DYER

2 July

The problem that we have with a victim mentality is that we forget to see the blessings of the day. Because of this, our spirit is poisoned instead of nourished.

STEVE MARABOLI, *Unapologetically You*

3 July

Any life truly lived is a risky business, and if one puts up too many fences against the risks one ends by shutting out life itself.

KENNETH S. DAVIS

4 July:
250th Anniversary of American Independence

There is some good in the worst of us and some evil in the best of us. When we discover this, we are less prone to hate our enemies.

MARTIN LUTHER KING JR, A Gift of Love

5 July

Count your blessings as the more you are grateful
for what you have the more there is to be grateful for.

PRAVIN AGARWAL

6 July

Gratitude transforms what you possess into all that
you need.

JENNIFER PIERRE

Now that we're half way through 2026, what are the moments that stand out for you?

7 July

Very little is needed to make a happy life; it is all within yourself, in your way of thinking.

MARCUS AURELIUS, *Meditations*

8 July

All love that has not friendship for its base,
Is like a mansion built upon the sand . . .
Love, to endure life's sorrow and earth's woe,
Needs friendship's solid masonwork below.

ELLA WHEELER WILCOX, *Poems of Passion*

9 July

You cannot have a positive life and a negative mind.

JOYCE MEYER, *Battlefield of the Mind*

10 July

The joy of life comes from our encounters with new experiences, and hence there is no greater joy than to have an endlessly changing horizon, for each day to have a new and different sun.

CHRISTOPHER MCCANDLESS, Letter to Ron Franz

11 July

A strong, positive self-image is the best possible preparation for success.

JOYCE BROTHERS

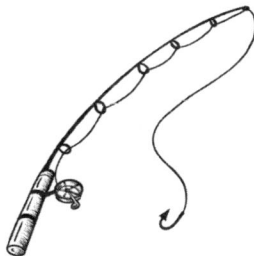

12 July

There is only one thing for us to do, and that is to do our level best right where we are every day of our lives; to use our best judgment, and then to trust the rest to that Power which holds the forces of the universe in his hands.

ORISON SWETT MARDEN, *The Optimistic Life*

13 July: *Bank Holiday in Northern Ireland*

Faith and prayer are the vitamins of the soul;
man cannot live in health without them.

MAHALIA JACKSON

14 July

Never be in a hurry; do everything quietly and in a calm spirit. Do not lose your inner peace for anything whatsoever, even if your whole world seems upset.

ST FRANCIS DE SALES, *Introduction to the Devout Life*

15 July

A grateful heart is a beginning of greatness. It is an expression of humility. It is a foundation for the development of such virtues as prayer, faith, courage, contentment, happiness, love, and well-being.

JAMES E. FAUST, 'Gratitude as a Saving Principle'

What are you grateful for?

16 July:
55th Anniversary of the Moon Landing

The higher we soar, the smaller we appear to those who cannot fly.

FRIEDRICH NIETZSCHE, *Thus Spoke Zarathustra*

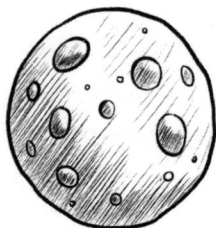

17 July

The secret of success is to be in harmony with existence, to be always calm to let each wave of life wash us a little farther up the shore.

CYRIL CONNOLLY

18 July

Never continue in a job you don't enjoy. If you're happy in what you're doing, you'll like yourself, you'll have inner peace. And if you have that, along with physical health, you will have had more success than you could possibly have imagined.

JOHNNY CARSON

19 July

Because I cannot do everything, I will not refuse to
do the something that I can do.

EDWARD EVERETT HALE

20 July

The trick to forgetting the big picture is to look at
everything close-up.

CHUCK PALAHNIUK, *Lullaby*

21 July

When faith is lost, when honor dies, the man is dead.

JOHN GREENLEAF WHITTIER, *Personal Poems*

22 July

The cucumber is bitter? Then throw it out.
There are brambles in the path? Then go around.
That's all you need to know.

MARCUS AURELIUS, Meditations

23 July

The day which we fear as our last is but the birthday of eternity.

SENECA, *Morals*

24 July

A life without love is like a year without summer.

Swedish Proverb

What do you love about summer?

25 July

Amid the turmoil and tumult of battle, there may be seeming disorder and yet no real disorder at all.

SUN TZU, The Art of War

26 July

I hasten to laugh at everything, for fear of being obliged to weep.

PIERRE BEAUMARCHAIS, The Barber of Seville

27 July

When you arise in the morning think of what a privilege it is to be alive, to think, to enjoy, to love.

MARCUS AURELIUS, Meditations

28 July

Dreams are today's answers to tomorrow's questions.

EDGAR CAYCE

29 July

Write it on your heart that every day is the best day
in the year.

RALPH WALDO EMERSON, *Society and Solitude*

30 July

The happiness of your life depends upon the quality of your thoughts.

MARCUS AURELIUS, *Meditations*

31 July

Feelings are much like waves: we can't stop them from coming, but we can choose which one to surf.

JONATAN MÅRTENSSON

Notes for July

August

Leonard Bernstein – *Chichester Psalms*

'To achieve great things, two things are needed;
a plan, and not quite enough time.'

LEONARD BERNSTEIN

I'm often asked by interviewers what the highlight of my working life has been and it's a question I find incredibly difficult to answer. I've been very fortunate to have enjoyed many stand-out moments in the forty-plus years I've been performing professionally.

As a boy treble, I travelled all over the world and met all kinds of interesting people, from royalty to A-listers, including Kermit the Frog and Roland Rat! But it's fair to say that no one I've met over the years has had as big a musical influence on me than the composer, conductor and pianist Leonard

Bernstein. He was an unparalleled musical giant and I got to hang out and perform with him!

I would argue that Leonard Bernstein was the greatest living composer when I met him. He was also one of the most important figures in the history of American classical music. A rare musician, he could easily have forged a successful career as a conductor, pianist or composer, but he chose to pursue all three – in addition to writing, teaching and broadcasting. He was born in Lawrence, Massachusetts, on 5 August 1918, the son of Jewish parents who immigrated to the US from Rivne, a city now located in western Ukraine. Although originally named Louis Bernstein, at the insistence of his grandparents, his parents called him Leonard, and shortly after his eighteenth birthday, he legally changed his name.

The young musician began teaching himself the piano aged ten when one was left at his family's house by his Aunt Clara. At first, his father, Clara's brother, attempted to discourage Bernstein's interest in the instrument by refusing to pay for any piano lessons but he eventually relented and Bernstein went on to study at two institutes renowned for their music programmes: Harvard College, where he achieved a Bachelor of Arts, graduating in 1939, and the Curtis Institute of Music, one of the world's top conservatoires. After leaving Curtis, Bernstein moved to New York City and changed the world of music for ever.

Bernstein had an ability to make classical music accessible to all. Often sitting at a great piano with a cigarette in hand, he made it all sound so simple. His legacy is monumental, spanning music, education and activism. As one of the most influential conductors of the twentieth century, Bernstein led the New York Philharmonic for over a decade and guest-conducted globally. He was the first American to conduct at La Scala opera house in Milan and his televised 'Young People's Concerts' introduced millions to the wonders of symphonic music, blending entertainment with deep educational value. A passionate humanist, Bernstein used his platform to advocate for civil rights, LGBTQ+ rights and global peace. His performances at pivotal moments – like conducting Beethoven's Symphony No. 9 in Berlin after the fall of the Wall – symbolised unity and hope.

Bernstein's compositions were ground-breaking, bridging classical and popular genres. His musical masterpiece, *West Side Story*, remains a cultural touchstone, celebrated for its vibrant fusion of jazz, Latin and classical styles. His symphonies ('Jeremiah', 'Age of Anxiety', 'Kaddish') and the operetta *Candide* further showcased his compositional versatility. He achieved an impressive array of distinctions during his career, including sixteen Grammy Awards, seven Emmys, two Tonys and a Kennedy Center Honour. Through his recordings, writings and mentorship of future musicians, Bernstein's influence endures. He combined unparalleled talent with a commitment to making music a transformative force in society and his work continues to inspire generations worldwide, especially his musical *West Side Story* which has inspired two films, released in both the twentieth and twenty-first centuries.

Bernstein announced that he would retire from conducting in 1990 at the age of seventy-two years old. He passed away five days after this announcement. I met him four years before he died when I was fifteen years old and at the height of my childhood fame, after three years of singing professionally. Even though my relatively short career had been littered with exciting job offers and numerous gold and platinum record awards, when the invitation came to work with Leonard Bernstein it blew my mind. It was a dream come true but I was also petrified!

One evening at home with mum and dad we watched a TV documentary about the making of Bernstein's musical, *West Side Story*, during which you could see that the great man had a fiery temper and was not afraid to use it. He annihilated the tenor José Carreras, shouting and ranting at him during a rehearsal. It was obvious Lenny was a perfectionist and José wasn't giving him what he wanted. (I should note here that Mr Bernstein, on viewing the footage of himself, wasn't aware at the time of how tough he had been on the tenor. It was obvious for everyone watching, though, that you never should mess with Leonard Bernstein.)

I made sure that I practised and practised the piece of music I was due to perform with him. It was called *Chichester Psalms* and it's described as a choral masterpiece blending Hebrew texts with vibrant harmonies and rhythms.

Combining lush orchestration, jazz influences and sacred tradition, *Chichester Psalms* has three movements evoking peace and spiritual triumph. Its lyrical melodies and complex textures reflect Bernstein's unique fusion of classical, modern and religious themes. It was the first time I had tackled Hebrew texts, and I spent hours memorising them phonetically.

The day came when I was due to meet the great man. I felt as prepared as was humanly possible as I had worked so hard. I was also very nervous; what if he turned on me like he had poor José? What if he hated my voice? What if he hated me? I was sitting in a rehearsal room in London's Barbican Hall, nervously biting my nails. The entire London Symphony Chorus lined one wall of the room while I sat alone on a chair opposite them. Suddenly the doors burst open and into the room walked this whirlwind of white hair, long black flowing velvet cloak and a bright red jumper. Leonard Bernstein walked over to me and put me in a headlock tapping me repeatedly on the head with his conductor's baton, saying, 'I've been wanting to work with you for ages!'. My brain was almost paralysed by an overwhelming mixture of fear and relief. My legs buckled beneath me and all I could think of was 'Leonard Bernstein's not supposed to say things like that!'. He seemed to be more like a friendly grandfather rather than a ranting ogre.

What followed was one of the greatest hours of my young life. Bernstein decided in that rehearsal room to give me my own personal masterclass in front of a hundred-strong chorus.

He said it was the last time for him to be able to get his piece sounding like it did in his head. He took me through the music, bar by bar, perfecting every second of it. He told me what to do and I did it! The atmosphere was electrifying. The hundred-strong chorus listened on silently and I was having the time of my life.

Chichester Psalms was unlike anything I had heard before; how could this complex modern piece have been written by the same person who wrote *West Side Story*? I could sense that the *Psalms* had come from deep within Bernstein's soul and that the music meant everything to him.

Bernstein had passion, heart and guts, and he is the greatest musician I have ever met and worked with. The energy he transmitted on stage was phenomenal: the minute he walked onto the platform he was completely transported into another world. I'd watch him dance on the podium, totally carried away by the music being made in front of him. He was always totally in control, with every eye in the orchestra and chorus transfixed on him. The energy coming from the tip of his baton was akin to Harry Potter's wand!

I performed three concerts with the great man and had the best time on and off stage. I learned more from watching him on stage than I ever have before or after. We hugged each other on stage and off after our final concert in Rome and that was the last time I ever saw him. We exchanged home phone numbers, and he asked me to give him a ring and sing for him

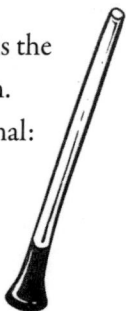

once my voice had broken. He died of a heart attack in his New York home not long after. He was buried next to his wife who had died twelve years previously.

According to Allen Shawn, the conductor's biographer, Bernstein was buried with a pocket score of Mahler's Symphony No. 5, a piece of amber, a lucky penny, a copy of *Alice in Wonderland* and a baton. I will fondly remember my special time with Leonard Bernstein for the rest of my life. And, who knows, when the inevitable time comes, I may well be buried with my copy of his *Chichester Psalms*.

> Yea, though I walk
> Through the valley of the shadow of death,
> I will fear no evil,
> For Thou art with me.

Psalm 23|:4

1 August

A genius in the wrong position could look like a fool.

IDOWU KOYENIKAN, Wealth for All

2 August

I think . . . if it is true that there are as many minds as there are heads, then there are as many kinds of love as there are hearts.

LEO TOLSTOY, *Anna Karenina*

3 August: *Bank Holiday in Scotland*

Nothing ventured, nothing gained.

GEOFFREY CHAUCER, *The Canterbury Tales*

4 August

God favors men and women who delight in being made worthy of happiness before the happiness itself.

CRISS JAMI, *Killosophy*

5 August

Don't wish . . . DO! Don't try . . . BE! Don't think . . . KNOW! And above all: Bless a stranger with a small, yet powerful, random act of kindness. You feel me?

T.F. HODGE, *From Within I Rise*

How could you bring kindness to the people in your life this month?

6 August

Don't count your blessings, let your blessings count!
Enjoy Life!

BERNARD KELVIN CLIVE

7 August

Birds that are useless for the table and not harmful
to the farm should always be preserved; and the
more beautiful they are, the more carefully they
should be preserved. They look a great deal better in
the swamps and on the beaches and among the trees
than they do on hats.

THEODORE ROOSEVELT in *The Outlook*, 1911

8 August

Practise what you preach and watch how life starts to work in your favour.

ROBIN S. BAKER

9 August

Be happy with what you have and are, be generous with both, and you won't have to hunt for happiness.

WILLIAM E. GLADSTONE

10 August

Great works are performed not by strength but by perseverance.

SAMUEL JOHNSON

11 August

I'm a success today because I had a friend who believed in me and I didn't have the heart to let him down.

ABRAHAM LINCOLN

12 August: *Total Solar Eclipse*

I was blessed with certain gifts and talents and
God gave them to me to be the best person I can be
and to have a positive impact on other people.

BRYAN CLAY

What talents and gifts can you share?

13 August

There is little difference in people, but that little
difference makes a big difference. The little difference
is attitude. The big difference is whether it is positive
or negative.

W. CLEMENT STONE

14 August

You cannot shake hands with a clenched fist.

INDIRA GANDHI

15 August

Good humor is a tonic for mind and body. It is the best antidote for anxiety and depression. It is a business asset. It attracts and keeps friends. It lightens human burdens. It is the direct route to serenity and contentment.

GRENVILLE KLEISER

16 August

It is difficult to say what is impossible, for the dream of yesterday is the hope of today and the reality of tomorrow.

ROBERT H. GODDARD

17 August

Let the beauty of what you love be what you do.

RUMI

18 August

There is no charm equal to tenderness of heart.

JANE AUSTEN, *Emma*

19 August

Lord, make me an instrument of thy peace.
Where there is hatred, let me sow love.

ST FRANCIS OF ASSISI, 'Peace Prayer'

20 August

If we have no peace, it is because we have
forgotten that we belong to each other.

MOTHER TERESA

21 August

Music is the shorthand of emotion.

LEO TOLSTOY

What are your favourite pieces of music?

22 August

Hope is like the sun which, as we journey towards it, casts the shadow of our burden behind us.

SAMUEL SMILES

23 August

It is better to know some of the questions than all of the answers.

JAMES THURBER, *A Thurber Carnival*

24 August

That's been one of my mantras – focus and simplicity.
Simple can be harder than complex: you have to work
hard to get your thinking clean to make it simple.
But it's worth it in the end because once you get there,
you can move mountains.

STEVE JOBS

25 August

If you want to go fast, go alone. If you want to go far, go together.

African Proverb

26 August

Shared joy is a double joy; shared sorrow is half a sorrow.

Swedish Proverb

27 August

Happiness is when what you think, what you say, and what you do are in harmony.

MAHATMA GANDHI

28 August

He who has a why to live for can bear almost any how.

FRIEDRICH NIETZSCHE,
Twilight of the Idols

29 August

Whether the weather be fine,
Or whether the weather be not,
Whether the weather be cold,
Or whether the weather be hot,
We'll weather the weather
Whatever the weather,
Whether we like it or not.

ANONYMOUS

30 August

As far as we can discern, the sole purpose of human existence is to kindle a light in the darkness of mere being.

CARL JUNG, *Memories, Dreams and Reflections*

31 August: *Bank Holiday*

It is the test of greatness in a person that he or she should be able to see greatness in others, and give them ungrudging credit for it.

JOHN RUSKIN

Notes for August

September

Antonin Dvorak – Symphony No. 9 in E minor, 'From the New World'

'Not everything is for everyone and not
everyone is for everything.'

ANTONIN DVORAK

Astronaut Neil Armstrong loved Antonin Dvorak's Symphony No. 9 so much, he literally took it to the Moon and back, because a tape of the piece accompanied him on the Apollo 11 mission, the first Moon landing in 1969.

Dvorak's symphony popularly known as the 'New World Symphony' was composed in 1893 while he was the director of the National Conservatory of Music in America. This is very much a symphony that looks back in time, from the USA to Dvorak's native Bohemia. He was the eldest of eight children, born in a small village north of Prague. A lover of folk

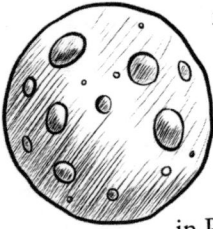

music from an early age, he even joined his dad in a local band. It was the lure of an amazing fee that persuaded Dvorak to venture to New York: he was offered twenty-five times what he was being paid in Prague – about £500,000 in today's money. No wonder he packed his bags and left!

From his house overlooking Stuyvesant Park in the Big Apple, he appeared to spend much of his time pining for Bohemia, rarely going out unless contractually obliged to do so, and taking every opportunity to remind himself of home. There were some American positives though: he was inspired by native American Music and the African American spirituals he had heard in the States; he was also inspired by the American landscape, including the prairies he saw on summer holidays spent with the Czech community in Iowa. Dvorak's 'New World Symphony' was premiered at Carnegie Hall in New York on 16 December 1893 and was met with great applause. The work launched a new era of American music and remains one of the best known and most loved symphonies of all time.

Dvorak and a young Aled Jones have something in common. It's not something I'm overly proud of, and it was only a fleeting thing. But we were both . . . trainspotters! As a nine-year-old boy Dvorak became intoxicated with the sight, sound and smell of steam locomotives. From then he never lost the opportunity to visit a railway station when he was on tour. This lifelong fascination reached its peak in America, when he would often ride New York's overhead railway and also watch passing trains from an embankment, even chatting with the drivers and the engineers. I swear I never went that far in my brief obsession, but when I was in my early teens and travelling a lot for work from North Wales down to London or Cardiff, I would jot down the numbers of passing trains. It was a perfect way to while away the time and eventually my book was full of rare and modern train numbers. For the record, I'm still on the lookout for the 92220 Evening Star (a preserved steam engine). The fact that Dvorak was also a spotter makes me feel a bit better about the whole thing.

I associate Dvorak's Symphony No. 9, 'From the New World', with a specific time in my life. In the 1970s an advert appeared on TV in the UK in which a young boy takes bread 'to the top of the world', to the soundtrack of Dvorak's tune. He's actually pushing a bike laden with loaves of bread up a very steep cobbled hill to Old Ma Beggaty's place. And here's a fun fact to impress your friends by the water cooler at work: this famed Hovis advert was directed by none other than Hollywood producer Ridley Scott. The music used in the advert is based on the second movement of Dvorak's Symphony No. 9. These days it's even got its own title called 'Going Home' and is a real favourite with listeners on the radio station Classic FM.

I remember this advert so vividly and the feeling it evoked in me. Its autumnal feel made me feel melancholic and nostalgic, searching back in my mind to past good times. It could easily have been the soundtrack to my walk back to school for the first day after the summer holidays. The drudge of the steep hill and hefty bread bike in the advert were replaced by my heavy heart and the weight of expectation of what lay ahead, as I reluctantly left the carefree joys of summer behind. I clung onto the memories of sunny adventures as every step brought me closer to a harsh reality of September.

Dvorak's masterpiece is performed nearly every year at the BBC Proms concerts at the Royal Albert Hall in London which is, as I've said, a very special venue for me, having sung there for the first time when I was only twelve years old. Apparently, I've appeared at the Hall over a hundred times in my career thus far. I felt especially honoured when I was included in artist Peter Blake's montage of 400 stars who've appeared most there. And if Dvorak's piece has an Autumnal feel that evokes memories of the past, then it's a perfect reminder of one of my favourite dates in my working diary. For over twenty years it felt very much like I was 'going home' when I presented the *Songs of Praise* 'Big Sing' at the Royal Albert Hall. We'd film our TV show the night after the Last Night of the Proms in September. The place would be packed with fans of the programme and the roof would be well and truly raised as 5,000 Christians

sang their hearts out. I was fortunate to sing solo most years, and I feel so privileged to have fronted that special occasion for so long.

It was during the filming of one of these shows that I experienced one of the biggest shocks of my life. I was mid-flow delivering what we call in the television industry a piece to camera (a short link introducing something to the people in the hall and those who will be watching on TV). As I was staring into the camera lens, I suddenly heard a soft murmur from the gathered audience, which got louder and louder, until everyone started cheering. I stopped in my tracks when I noticed that I'd been joined on stage by the broadcaster Michael Aspel, a 'big red book' in his hands. He delivered the words I never thought I'd hear: 'Aled Jones . . . This is your life!' (*This Is Your Life* was a biographical TV show where a guest was caught unawares and taken through their life story with appearances from family, friends and notable figures.) They say God moves in mysterious ways; at the precise moment when I was surprised by Michael, God was definitely with me, because he helped me not to swear in front of the audience! Otherwise, I would have been 'Going Home' with my tail firmly between my legs!

1 September

Gratitude bestows reverence . . . changing
forever how we experience life and the world.

JOHN MILTON

2 September

You are human and mortal; we are the sum
of our weak moments and our strong.

MERCEDES LACKEY, *The Black Gryphon*

3 September

Those blessings are sweetest that are won with prayer and worn with thanks.

THOMAS GOODWIN, 'A Discourse of Thankfulness'

4 September

Sometimes we focus so much on what we don't have that we fail to see, appreciate, and use what we do have!

JEFF DIXON

5 September

The soul which has no fixed purpose in life is lost; to be everywhere, is to be nowhere.

MICHEL DE MONTAIGNE

September can be a season of new beginnings.
Are there new opportunities you could take?

6 September

Burning bridges behind you is understandable.
It's the bridges before us that we burn, not realizing
we may need to cross, that brings regret.

ANTHONY LICCIONE

7 September

God can take the ordinary and create the
extraordinary. Our incredible God has the power
to transform your simple life and give you the life
of your dreams. Remarkable things happen in your
life when you believe.

AMAKA IMANI NKOSAZANA, *Heart Crush*

8 September

A good laugh is sunshine in the house.

WILLIAM MAKEPEACE THACKERAY,
Sketches and Travels in London

9 September

Your purpose in life is to find your purpose and
give your whole heart and soul to it.

BUDDHA

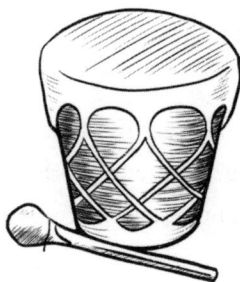

10 September

'What makes the desert beautiful,' said the little
prince, 'is that somewhere it hides a well.'

ANTOINE DE SAINT-EXUPÉRY,
The Little Prince

11 September

If, when stung by slander or ill-nature, we wax proud
and swell with anger, it is a proof that our gentleness
and humility are unreal, and mere artificial show.

ST FRANCIS DE SALES,
Introduction to the Devout Life

12 September

Peace is not a relationship of nations. It is a condition of mind brought about by a serenity of soul. Peace is not merely the absence of war. It is also a state of mind. Lasting peace can come only to peaceful people.

JAWAHARLAL NEHRU

Who are the peacemakers in your life?

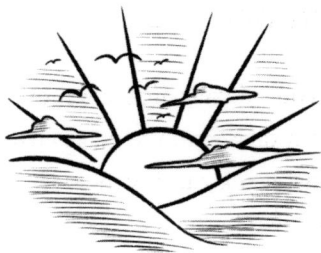

13 September

Always remember that you are absolutely unique.
Just like everyone else.

MARGARET MEAD

14 September

Getting stress out of your life takes more than prayer alone. You must take action to make changes and stop doing whatever is causing the stress. You can learn to calm down in the way you handle things.

JOYCE MEYER, Starting Your Day Right

15 September

The Fates guide the person who accepts them and hinder the person who resists them.

CLEANTHES

16 September

Life itself is the most wonderful fairy tale.

HANS CHRISTIAN ANDERSEN

17 September

The future belongs to those who believe in the beauty of their dreams.

ELEANOR ROOSEVELT

18 September

I will not follow where the path may lead, but I will go where there is no path, and I will leave a trail.

MURIEL STRODE, 'Wind-Wafted Wild Flowers'

19 September

Whoever cannot seek the unforeseen sees nothing, for the known way is an impasse.

HERACLITUS, *Fragments*

20 September

Above all, remember that God looks for solid virtues in us, such as patience, humility, obedience, abnegation of your own will – that is, the good will to serve Him and our neighbour in Him. His providence allows us other devotions only insofar as He sees that they are useful to us.

SAINT IGNATIUS,
Letter to Father Philip Leernus, 1553

How could you help a neighbour
this season?

21 September: *Yom Kippur*

Never forget the three powerful resources you always
have available to you: love, prayer, and forgiveness.

H. JACKSON BROWN JR,
Life's Instructions for Wisdom, Success, and Happiness

22 September: *Autumn Equinox*

You'll have time to rest when you're dead.

ROBERT DE NIRO

23 September

Throw your dreams into space like a kite, and you do not know what it will bring back, a new life, a new friend, a new love, a new country.

ANAÏS NIN, The Diary of Anaïs Nin

24 September

What you see in yourself is what you see in the world.

Afghan Proverb

25 September

Holding on is believing that there's only a past; letting go is knowing that there's a future.

DAPHNE ROSE KINGMA,
The Ten Things to Do When Your Life Falls Apart

26 September

The first step towards getting somewhere is
to decide you're not going to stay where you are.

J.P. MORGAN

27 September

Imagination has brought mankind through the dark ages to its present state of civilization. Imagination led Columbus to discover America. Imagination led Franklin to discover electricity. Imagination has given us the steam engine, the telephone, the talking-machine, and the automobile, for these things had to be dreamed of before they became realities.

L. FRANK BAUM, *The Lost Princess of Oz*

28 September

When you are offended at any person's fault, turn
to yourself and study your own failings. Then you
will forget your anger.

EPICTETUS, *Discourses*

29 September

Today, let us make haste to enjoy life. Who knows
if we will be tomorrow?

JEAN RACINE, *Athalie*

30 September

If only. Those must be the two saddest
words in the world.

MERCEDES LACKY

Notes for September

October

Ralph Vaughan Williams –
The Lark Ascending

'The art of music above all the other arts is the
expression of the soul of a nation.'

RALPH VAUGHAN WILLIAMS

As my friend Cerys Matthews once sang, 'Every day
when I wake up, I thank the Lord I'm Welsh.' The Cata-
tonia rock-group singer and I were both born and brought
up in a country where music was very much the soul of
the nation. Wales is called the 'Land of Song' for a reason.
All my lessons at school included music and singing, even
maths and geography; the teachers didn't need an excuse to
get the guitar out! As young children we were encouraged
to perform, usually at Eisteddfods, which are unique Welsh
festivals of literature, music and performance, celebrating

the country's rich cultural heritage. The term comes from the Welsh word 'eistedd' (meaning 'to sit') and originally referred to gatherings of poets and musicians competing in bardic contests.

Eisteddfods take place all the time in Wales and range in size and stature from tiny local ones held in chapels to international ones that draw people from all over the world, like the very famous one in Llangollen. The two main Eisteddfods for me growing up were the Urdd ones and the National.

The National Eisteddfod is a competition for young people and adults alike, held once a year and showcasing the best of the best in Wales. The whole week of competitions is televised and shown on Welsh TV. The Urdd ones are for the younger generation: 'Urdd Gobaith Cymru' (often just called the Urdd) is a Welsh youth organisation that promotes Welsh language, culture and identity through activities, sports and the arts. It was founded in 1922 and is one of the largest youth movements in Europe, with thousands of members across Wales. To get to the Urdd Eisteddfod final, held somewhere in South Wales and North Wales alternatively, you would have to win your category (solo singing in my case) locally and county-wide first. It was a big thing in schools across Wales and the competition was fierce. I won the Under 12 solo singing competition once, but I didn't make it onto TV because the Pope was visiting Wales the same day and the TV producers obviously thought he was bigger news than me! My father was rather upset!

I only competed in the National Eisteddfod once. It happened to be the same year as the release of my first album in Wales. I didn't even make the top three finalists (that's what you call a real leveller!). I am, though, so thankful that I had these Eisteddfods in my life when I was growing up, because they taught me how to perform and engage with an audience. And they taught me how to accept defeat graciously (I still struggle with this!). I do believe that children in Wales have a head start on children anywhere else when it comes to performing, and that's thanks to these Eisteddfods.

These cultural events also help promote our precious language. I love the fact that I'm fluent in Welsh; in fact, I couldn't speak English until I was about four years old. So English is very much my second language. Since 15 October 2013 there has been a special day set aside to promote the Welsh language, a day to encourage people to start every conversation with 'Shwmae or Su'mae?', which means 'How's it going?' in South Walian and North Walian respectively. On 15 October the people are encouraged to celebrate the Welsh language in their community, workplace, school or college.

It's open to everyone, wherever you are, whatever your age, and you don't need to be able to speak Welsh fluently to take part. The event aims to show that the Welsh language belongs to us all – fluent speakers, learners or those shy about their Welsh. So, on the fifteenth of this month if someone comes up to you and asks 'Shwmae or Su'mae?', all you need to do is answer 'Da iawn, diolch!', which means 'Very good, thanks!'. Go on! Give it a go!

I'm a big fan of Vaughan Williams' music, and as a Welshman I have him to thank, in part, for promoting our fabulous Welsh hymns. Even though Vaughan Williams was an Englishman, born in Down Ampney in Gloucestershire on 12 October 1872, and was held in high regard as a composer of symphonies, choral works and folk songs, he also arranged some of our Welsh hymn tunes for *The English Hymnal* – hymns like 'Cwm Rhondda', 'Hyfrydol' and 'Rhosymedre' (more commonly known as 'Guide Me, O Thou Great Redeemer', 'Love Divine, All Loves Excelling' and 'Immortal, Invisible').

These arrangements reflect his deep appreciation of the rich musical heritage of Wales. His work on *The English Hymnal* was instrumental in bringing Welsh music into the broader British choral tradition. I play his orchestral arrangement of the Welsh hymn 'Rhosymedre' often on Classic FM and always shed a nostalgic tear! Rhosymedre is a small village, around four miles from Wrexham and not far from the picturesque Denbighshire Hills. The area offers stunning views, particularly towards the Clywedog Valley and the hills of Snowdonia further west. It is a peaceful, quiet village, ideal for nature lovers and those seeking a rural setting.

Rhosymedre would have been the perfect setting too to inspire what has become Vaughan Williams' biggest hit. His piece *The Lark Ascending* was, instead, inspired by Victorian English poet and novelist George Meredith's poem of the same name, which celebrates the flight of the skylark as a symbol of freedom, beauty and transcendence. The poem, written in 1881, is a lengthy and detailed depiction of the lark's song and movement, emphasising its joy and ethereal quality. It comes from Meredith's book, *Poems and Lyrics of the Joy of Earth*.

Although not directly composed with October in mind, *The Lark Ascending* is often linked to the tranquil, reflective atmosphere of autumn. This piece, evoking the image of a lark soaring over the English countryside, carries a certain nostalgic quality that resonates with the melancholy often felt around this time of year. The subtle beauty and calmness of the music convey the fading light as the clocks go back, the nights gather in as autumn deepens and nature adorns itself in shades of gold, amber and crimson – colours that are frequently associated with October. Ralph Vaughan Williams originally composed the piece for violin and piano in 1914 and then reworked it for violin and orchestra after the First World War. The orchestral and solo violin version is what I play on the radio.

There's a running joke in the classical music industry that when you hear *The Lark Ascending* played on the radio, it usually means that the presenter either needed an extended loo break or to nip out of the studio to get a coffee or a cup of tea. It's about fifteen minutes in duration from start to finish! I play it often on my shows on Classic FM because it's a very popular piece, and I like it very much. Do I leave the studio for sustenance, or to use the loo, while it's playing? 'Wrth gwrs, oni fyddech chi?!', as we say in Wales. There's another phrase for you to try out on 15 October: Shwmae/Su'mae Day. It means, in Welsh, 'Of course, wouldn't you?!'.

1 October

You're not weak because you can't read. You're weak because you're afraid of people seeing your weakness. You're letting shame decide who you are.

LEIGH BARDUGO, *Crooked Kingdom*

2 October

Press forward. Do not stop, do not linger in your journey, but strive for the mark set before you.

GEORGE WHITEFIELD

3 October

If you look for perfection, you'll never be content.

LEO TOLSTOY, *Anna Karenina*

4 October: *Grandparents' Day*

Tell me and I forget, teach me and I may remember,
involve me and I learn.

XUN KUANG, *Xunzi*

5 October

In the end, life is about collecting experiences and
looking for the lesson and blessing in each one. Yet we
are never to carry these experiences on our backs, only
in our hearts. One will hold us back, while the other
will keep us moving forward.

SUZY KASSEM, *Rise Up and Salute the Sun*

What are some important experiences and lessons you carry?

6 October

God will exceed your expectations; He will answer your prayers and shower you with many blessings. Pray and believe.

GIFT GUGU MONA, *Prayer: An Antidote for the Inner Man*

7 October

Even a happy life cannot be without a measure of darkness, and the word happy would lose its meaning if it were not balanced by sadness. It is far better to take things as they come along with patience and equanimity.

CARL JUNG in 'The Art of Living', *Sunday Times*, 1960

8 October

Our whole way of life today is dedicated to the removal of risk. Cradle to grave we are supported, insulated, and isolated from the risks of life.

SHIRLEY TEMPLE BLACK

9 October

It's your outlook on life that counts. If you take yourself lightly and don't take yourself too seriously, pretty soon you can find the humor in our everyday lives. And sometimes it can be a lifesaver.

BETTY WHITE

10 October

Chaotic people often have chaotic lives, and I think they create that. But if you try and have an inner peace and a positive attitude, I think you attract that.

IMELDA STAUNTON

11 October

The happiness of this life depends less on what befalls you than the way in which you take it.

ELBERT HUBBARD

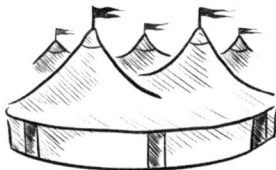

12 October

If they're not talking about you, you're not doing
something; you're not doing anything. So if they're
talking about you, you may be doing something right.
And when they talk bad about you, you just use it
for motivation.

PAUL PIERCE

Who are the people you enjoy talking with?
Take a moment to reflect on why you enjoy
talking with them.

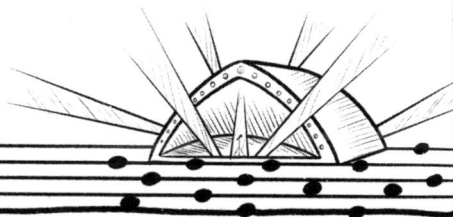

13 October

Serenity is the balance between good and bad, life and death, horrors and pleasures. Life is, as it were, defined by death. If there wasn't death of things, then there wouldn't be any life to celebrate.

NORMAN DAVIES

14 October

To truly laugh, you must be able to take your pain, and play with it!

CHARLIE CHAPLIN

15 October

Man does not simply exist, but always decides what his existence will be, what he will become the next moment. By the same token, every human being has the freedom to change at any instant.

VICTOR FRANKL, *Man's Search For Meaning*

16 October

The only true wisdom is in knowing you know nothing.

SOCRATES, *Plato's Apology*

17 October

The most difficult thing is the decision to act,
the rest is merely tenacity. The fears are paper tigers.
You can do anything you decide to do. You can act
to change and control your life; and the procedure,
the process is its own reward.

AMELIA EARHART

Are there things that you need to take action on?

18 October

How many are the pains of those who hunger for revenge! They gnaw away at themselves constantly, and they have killed themselves even before they kill their enemies.

CATHERINE OF SIENA, *The Dialogue*

19 October

But the law of loving others could not be discovered by reason, because it is unreasonable.

LEO TOLSTOY, *Anna Karenina*

20 October

I am ready to meet my Maker. Whether my Maker is prepared for the great ordeal of meeting me is another matter.

WINSTON CHURCHILL, London, 30 November 1949

21 October

Although love dwells in gorgeous palaces, and sumptuous apartments, more willingly than in miserable and desolate cottages, it cannot be denied but that he sometimes causes his power to be felt in the gloomy recesses of forests, among the most bleak and rugged mountains, and in the dreary caves of a desert.

GIOVANNI BOCCACCIO, *The Decameron*

22 October

Change yourself and fortune will change.

Portuguese Proverb

23 October

The things you think about determine the quality of your mind. Your soul takes on the colour of your thoughts.

MARCUS AURELIUS, *Meditations*

24 October

When a friend, then, indulges in the joy of unburdening a secret on to another friend's bosom, he makes the latter, in his turn, feel the urge to taste the same joy himself.

ALESSANDRO MANZONI, *The Betrothed*

25 October: *Clocks Go Back*

Be like a duck. Calm on the surface, but always paddling like the dickens underneath.

MICHAEL CAINE

26 October

Never stand begging for that which you have the power to earn.

MIGUEL DE CERVANTES, *Don Quixote*

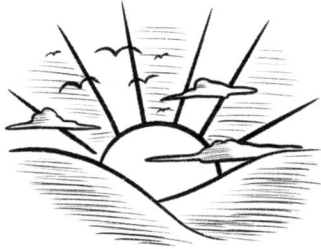

27 October

Life must be lived forward, but it can only be understood backwards.

SØREN KIERKEGAARD, *Journal*

28 October

The only thing that can stop you is the doubt that you carry in your mind.

WILLIAM C. RICHARDSON

29 October

If the only miracle we are looking for is the big one . . .
then we will most likely miss the other miracles that are
unfolding before our very eyes, each and every day.

JYOTI PRAKASH DASH,
My Encounter with Cancer

30 October

Patience is a conquering virtue.

GEOFFREY CHAUCER

31 October: *Halloween*

I do not feel obliged to believe that the same God who has endowed us with senses, reason, and intellect has intended us to forgo their use and by some other means to give us knowledge which we can attain by them.

GALILEO GALILEI,
Letter to the Grand Duchess Christina, 1615

Notes for October

November

William Mathias –
Let the People Praise Thee, O God

May God be gracious to us and bless us
and make his face shine on us –
so that your ways may be known on earth,
your salvation among all nations.

Psalm 67:1–2

November is a month of remembrance, a time when the world pauses to honour those who made the ulti-mate sacrifice. On the eleventh hour of the eleventh day of the eleventh month, we mark Armistice Day, now known as Remembrance Day, commemorating the end of the First World War in 1918. Poppies bloom on lapels as symbols of bloodshed and resilience, inspired by the haunting words of John McCrae's poem 'In Flanders Fields'. Across nations, silent vigils, solemn parades and heartfelt tributes unite people in gratitude. It is a time to reflect not only on those lost in past conflicts but also on the enduring impact of war on families, communities and history, and lends the opportunity to pray for peace and healing in our world. I've been honoured through my role as a presenter on *Songs of Praise* to interview veterans and have always found them so inspiring. Although I have always believed that one should remember for more than just a day, it's good to have a special day to reflect and give thanks.

The month of November is also important in the history of Welsh music as one of our greatest composers, William Mathias, was born on 1 November 1934. My first introduction to Mathias' music came in 1981 when I was a young chorister at Bangor Cathedral. I would have been ten years old and would have just moved up in rank from being a lowly probationer. The thrill of being in the main choir was like nothing I had experienced: I was finally singing with 'the big boys' and I was on cloud nine! I remember being so proud when I sang my first service without singing a note out of place.

So, 1981 was a big year for me, but it was a monumental year in the history of the United Kingdom too. Even though I lived on the Island of Anglesey in North Wales, and the rest of the country hardly knew we existed, we still kept in touch with the news, and were, like the rest of the world, captivated by the impending wedding of Prince Charles and Lady Diana

Spencer. We also had an interest because one of our own was involved in the grand occasion: there had been a buzz in the Welsh press for some time regarding local composer William Mathias, who had been commissioned to write the anthem for the actual wedding service. And it wasn't just the Welsh press who were reporting on it. This is how the *New York Times* announced the news:

> The first music that Prince Charles and Lady Diana will hear after they are married next Wednesday in St Paul's Cathedral will not be a work that has long been part of the liturgy but a new anthem by William Mathias, commissioned by the Prince for the occasion. The invitation was conveyed to Mr Mathias, a professor of music at University College of North Wales, by Sir David Willcocks, who is directing the music for the wedding.
>
> The anthem, *Let the People Praise Thee, O God*, is a setting of Psalm 67 for chorus and organ, and lasts about four minutes.

If the truth be known, we choristers at Bangor were quite envious of our contemporaries at St Paul's Cathedral. To put it into perspective, you could fit around five Bangor Cathedrals into St Paul's, hence the chips we carried around on our shoulders; they were the untouchables and we were the mere pretenders . . . at least, that's how we saw it! There had been so much talk about the music for the wedding in our little rehearsal room at Bangor. By all accounts the boys at St Paul's were rehearsing all day, every day, so that they were perfect for the big day. Apparently, they were being paid a fortune too!

A few weeks before the wedding, I remember walking up the big stone staircase to our rehearsal room, the smell of the Calor gas heater getting stronger and stronger with every step. When I entered the room, with rows of chairs circling a big grand piano, and took my seat, I could hear a lot of excited chatter coming from the older boys. Apparently, Mr Goodwin, our choirmaster, had an exciting announcement to make.

When he walked into the room we instantly fell silent. He went on to explain that the composer William Mathias had finished his anthem for the Royal Wedding and was keen to hear it being performed. He would like us to learn it and perform it in a Thursday Evensong in a week's time. The room erupted in a deafening roar of cheers, fists pumping the air, voices rising in exhilaration. But then, like a wave receding, the energy shifted. A few of us exchanged nervous glances, excitement giving way to doubt. Could we really do this? Were we good enough? Of all the people they could have chosen, why us? Mr Goodwin asked: 'So, are you all up for the challenge?', and once again we all cheered enthusiastically. I could feel my heart pumping in my chest. Yes, there was a big Royal Wedding taking place in London involving one of the best choirs in the world, but our little choir, hundreds of miles away in North Wales, was also playing a part. A huge part! We were testing the music before the world got to hear it; this new music was being sung by us first. That made us feel so special and I, for one, went home to mum and dad bursting with pride and excitement.

William Mathias' composition, *Let the People Praise Thee, O God*, is a jubilant and majestic choral work based on Psalm 67. It was the hardest piece of music I'd ever sung and I found it so difficult to learn. It showcases his signature rhythmic vitality, rich harmonies and grand orchestration, and it was unlike anything I'd seen before. We practised harder than ever and eventually had it sounding resplendent.

The following Thursday at just after 5.00pm we processed into our cathedral. There were only three people in the congregation. I felt so deflated: the fact that we were singing to an almost empty house was so demoralising. But then I noticed a lone figure creeping into the back of the cathedral and sitting down, his raincoat collar pulled high around his ears and a big Russian hat on his head. My heart stopped and I felt a flush of emotion. It was William Mathias – the composer himself had come to hear his anthem being performed for the very first time. To say I was elated would be the greatest understatement ever and I sang my heart out, as did the rest of the choir. As the anthem concluded we all looked to the back of the congregation when Mr Mathias stood up and mimed a round of applause.

The following week on 29 July, I, along with almost a billion people, watched the St Paul's Cathedral Choir sing a brand-new anthem composed by William Mathias, especially for the Royal Wedding of Prince Charles and Lady Diana Spencer. The choir, of course, sang it beautifully – a much better performance than we had given, if truth be told. But I watched on bursting with pride, knowing that I had sung this special piece of music before anyone else!

Little did I know, back then, that William and his wife Yvonne would become firm friends and two people who would shape my future career. William was a man of exceptional energy. Warm and generous in character, he lived several different kinds of musical lives. First and foremost, a composer, he was also a conductor, pianist, public figure, Professor of Music at Bangor University and Artistic Director of the North Wales Music Festival. His wife Yvonne was head of singing at the University, and it's in this capacity that I got to work with her.

I decided after leaving school to audition for a place at the Royal Academy of Music in London. Even though I had been singing all my life, I was keen to enrol as a singing student there and Yvonne agreed to help me prepare for the audition. She was a brilliant teacher and especially good with me, as my adult voice was very young and immature. She was a larger-than-life character and incredibly kind, and I adored our lessons on a Sunday morning when I'd arrive at the Mathias' house in the town of Menai Bridge, on the beautiful

Isle of Anglesey, just after 10.30am and every week without fail I'd see William hard at work in his study, black ink being put down on a manuscript.

Occasionally, during our lessons, he would walk in and offer to play the piano and give advice. On those occasions the lessons descended into fits of giggles as the three of us would sing and dance around. He once declaimed from the piano that the only thing that would make my voice and performance better would be a large gin and tonic, and Yvonne was promptly dispatched to the kitchen, returning with three fishbowls in hand.

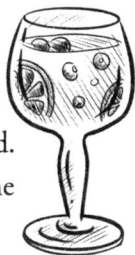

I am so thankful to Yvonne and William for the care they took of me at that crucial time in my development. They were so kind and full of fun and and made learning such a pleasure. They were both thrilled when I passed my audition and gained my place at the Royal Academy.

So, this 1 November, on what would be William's birth-day, I will fondly remember them both and my small role as part of one of the most-watched weddings in history.

1 November: *All Saints' Day*

Where words fail, music speaks.

HANS CHRISTIAN ANDERSEN

2 November

Music washes away from the soul the dust of
everyday life.

BERTHOLD AUERBACH, *On the Heights*

3 November

There are four ways God answers prayer:

No, not yet;
No, I love you too much;
Yes, I thought you'd never ask;
Yes, and here's more.

ANNE LEWIS

4 November

Appreciation is like an insurance policy.
It has to be renewed every now and then.

DAVE MCINTYRE

In this season of remembering, who are the people who helped shape who are you today?

5 November: *Guy Fawkes' Day*

Blessed is he who has learned to admire but not envy,
to follow but not imitate, to praise but not flatter,
and to lead but not manipulate.

WILLIAM ARTHUR WARD

6 November

If we can give up our self-centered concerns and see that this world doesn't exist only to satisfy our desires, then just as in begging, we cannot help but appreciate the things we receive as blessings.

KOSHO UCHIYAMA ROSHI,
The Zen Teaching of Homeless Kodo

7 November

Let us be grateful to people who make us happy, they are the charming gardeners who make our souls blossom.

MARCEL PROUST, *Pleasures and Regrets*

8 November: *Remembrance Sunday*

From failing hands we throw the torch to you,
be yours to hold it high.

JOHN MCRAE, 'In Flanders Fields'

9 November

Curiosity endows the people who have it with a generosity in argument and a serenity in their own mode of life which springs from their cheerful willingness to let life take the form it will.

ALISTAIR COOKE

10 November

The truest way to be deceived is to think oneself more knowing than others.

FRANÇOIS DE LA ROCHEFOUCAULD,
Maxims

11 November: *Armistice Day*

The best revenge is to be unlike him who performed the injury.

MARCUS AURELIUS, Meditations

12 November

The best way to find yourself is to lose yourself
in the service of others.

MAHATMA GANDHI

13 November

Do you know when you may concede your
insignificance? Before God or, perhaps, before
the intellect, beauty, or nature, but not before
people. Among people, one must be conscious
of one's dignity.

ANTON CHEKHOV,
Letter to his brother M.P. Chekhov

14 November

The person who can bring the spirit of laughter into a room is indeed blessed.

BENNETT CERF

Who makes you laugh?

15 November

Any concern too small to be turned into a
prayer is too small to be made into a burden.

CORRIE TEN BOOM,
Clippings From my Notebook

16 November

With faith, discipline and selfless devotion to duty,
there is nothing worthwhile that you cannot achieve.

MUHAMMAD ALI JINNAH

17 November

True strength lies in submission which permits one
to dedicate his life, through devotion, to something
beyond himself.

HENRY MILLER, *The Time of the Assassins*

18 November

Good judgment comes from experience, and a lot of that comes from bad judgment.

WILL ROGERS

19 November: *International Men's Day*

If a man has not discovered something that he will die for, he isn't fit to live.

MARTIN LUTHER KING JR, Detroit, 1963

20 November

Don't send me flowers when I'm dead. If you like me, send them while I'm alive.

BRIAN CLOUGH

21 November

Healing takes courage, and we all have courage,
even if we have to dig a little to find it.

TORI AMOS

22 November

Where love reigns, the impossible may be attained.

Indian Proverb

What are the 'impossible' things you'd
love to see?

23 November

You're only given a little spark of madness and
if you lose that, you're nothing.

ROBIN WILLIAMS, Live at the Roxy, 1978

24 November

Happiness depends upon ourselves.

ARISTOTLE

25 November

Thankfulness brings you to the place where the Beloved lives.

RUMI

26 November

The life each of us lives is the life within the limits of our own thinking. To have life more abundant, we must think in the limitless terms of abundance.

THOMAS DREIER

27 November

Delay always breeds danger; and to protract a great design is often to ruin it.

MIGUEL DE CERVANTES, Don Quixote

28 November

We can know nothing of humankind without knowing something of ourselves. Self-knowledge is the property of those people whose passions have their full play, but who ponder over their results.

BENJAMIN DISRAELI

29 November: *Start of Advent*

I believe in the imagination. What I cannot see is
infinitely more important than what I can see.

DUANE MICHALS, *Real Dreams*

30 November: *St Andrew's Day*

Absence diminishes small loves and increases
great ones, as the wind blows out the candle and
fans the bonfire.

FRANÇOIS DUC DE LA ROCHEFOUCAULD,
Maxims

Notes for November

December

Charles Wesley –
'Hark! The Herald Angels Sing'

'The greatest gifts are not wrapped in paper but in love.'

ANONYMOUS

The first time I became aware of my voice giving pleasure to others was at my grandparents' homes. Whenever I visited them, which was most weekends, I was encouraged to sing. Sometimes standing next to the piano, sometimes even standing on the dining table. My performances were always met with huge applause and shouts of Bravo! or 'Da iawn!', which is 'Well done!' in Welsh.

Christmas in both grandparents' homes was a special time and always filled with music and dancing. My mother's parents were into the popular tunes of the time – artists like Bing Crosby, Andy Williams and Elvis, which they'd listen to on

vinyl records played on a massive record player that was the size of a sideboard. My father's parents loved their traditional music more, so I usually sang the Welsh hymns with them, and at Christmas both Welsh and English carols were often belted out heartily. When I sang, I was handed a big white plate with a slab of homemade Christmas cake on it; my father's mother loved to cook, and loved to feed! I didn't care much for the fruity filling of the cake, but I adored the thick marzipan and icing. I realised very early on that the more I sang, the bigger the slice of cake!

Grandparents (or 'nain and taid' as we call them in North Wales), were the light of my life. Mine were called after where they lived: nain and taid 'Caernarfon' were my mum's parents and they lived in the seaside town of Caernarfon; nain and taid 'Llanwnda' were my dad's parents who lived a few miles outside Caernarfon in a tiny village called Llanwnda. My mum's parents were called Emrys and Annie and they loved each other so much – taid a builder and nain a housewife who was a diabetes type 1 sufferer. The first time I ever saw a needle was in her hand, a huge metal one that she'd stick in her leg or arm twice a day. I felt so sorry for her, but it never seemed to get her down; it was a way of life for her, and she was never far away from a barley sugar sweet, which I occasionally got to eat too. My

nain was a lovely woman with a huge heart, always making me laugh and playing the piano. Taid had a huge jar of sweets next to his armchair – usually 'Liquorice Allsorts' and white, yellow and pink bon bons. I loved sticking my hand in that jar; in fact, it was so large I could get my whole arm in and very often I was caught out by my mum, with my arm halfway in or halfway out.

My treat when I went round to their house, was a pack of Harbutt's modelling plasticine. It had seven different colours and was advertised on the cardboard container as being 'a pack full of fun'. And it certainly was (that's after being warned with the usual 'death threat' from mum if I got any of it on the carpet or sofa!). Taid could model anything from that plasticine, and I adored the time we spent together, me sitting on his lap in his armchair. He'd model animals, cars, people . . . you name it, he could build it. And then I'd get to squish it all together and mix all the colours into a huge multicoloured ball.

My father's parents, Jack and Violet, or 'nain and taid Llanwnda', were quieter and more introverted but equally loving and kind. My gran spoilt me rotten and we loved playing games, cooking and exploring. With my grandad I often sang hymns while sitting on his lap on his rocking chair, and I felt on top of the world when I was on that chair. He and his brothers sang in choirs, had great voices and loved to sing at any opportunity. He was a very practical man, and I loved chopping logs with him in their little yard, using my special axe. Unbeknown to me, he made sure it was so blunt it couldn't damage me, but I thought I was incredibly grown up using it. His skills were handed down to my father who is equally brilliant at practical things (for the record, I'm not too bad at DIY either, but nowhere near as good as taid and dad).

In both homes Christmas carols were such an important part of celebrations. My grandparents adored it when I sang a Christmas carol, and I certainly enjoyed singing with them from as far back as I can remember. The moment I started learning those carols, I realised that I had become part of a long and special tradition. It was as if we were being handed a precious gift, a song that our grandparents would have sung when they were very young too. It was just so magical; letting these songs seep into my soul changed my life. The carols have remained a part of me ever since.

I also found out early on that the act of singing these festive tunes every December had a remarkable effect on my mood. It's only as I got older I learnt that the positive feelings that arise from singing them can be attributed to several psychological, emotional and physiological factors that combine to create a sense of well-being. These songs are often joyful, upbeat and associated with themes of love, peace and celebration. When we sing, our brains release 'feel-good' chemicals such as dopamine and endorphins, which improve our mood and reduce feelings of stress. The rhythm and melody of the carols have the power to lift our spirits, creating a sense of euphoria and excitement that is hard to replicate in other activities. From childhood to the present day, I've loved the threads of community and connection singing these pieces fosters. We can't help but feel a sense of unity and belonging, reminding us that we are part of something greater than ourselves.

The hymn and carol writers obviously felt this deep connection too, and in December we should give thanks to God for the hymn and carol writer Charles Wesley – I know I do! He was such an influential English hymn writer and preacher, born on 21 December in 1707. He is best known for composing over 6,500 hymns, many of which are still sung in churches all over the world today. What a staggering achievement!

Wesley's hymns, such as 'O for a Thousand Tongues to Sing' and 'Love Divine, All Loves Excelling', focus on themes of faith, love and the Christian journey, with a healthy dollop of celebration. Charles Wesley was a key figure in the Methodist movement, which was founded by his brother, John Wesley. The Methodist movement emphasised personal faith, holiness, social justice and spreading Christianity through preaching and hymns. Charles Wesley's hymns helped spread the message of Christianity in a way that was both accessible and inspiring. We have him to thank for one of our most popular carols too. Imagine a festive season without a hearty rendition of 'Hark! The Herald Angels Sing' – Wesley's words at their finest, full of glory, hope, joy and adoration. I find it thrilling and always let rip on the last verse descant.

My grandparents never got to witness my success as a boy soprano and I often wonder how they would have reacted to it all – probably with unadulterated joy and pride. I am, though, so glad of those little impromptu performances I gave especially for them when I was a child. They saw me up close and personal, warts and all, which was even more special.

So, this Christmas, whether you're celebrating with friends, strangers, family or even enjoying a tabletop performance from children or grandchildren, be safe in the knowledge that the act of sharing the joy of music can brighten spirits and leave one with lasting feelings of happiness and goodwill.

> Joyful, all ye nations, rise,
> Join the triumph of the skies;
> With angelic hosts proclaim,
> 'Christ is born in Bethlehem.'

1 December

It is one of my sources of happiness never to desire
a knowledge of other people's business.

DOLLEY MADISON,
Life and Letters of Dolly Madison

2 December

Faith is an excitement and an enthusiasm; it is a
condition of intellectual magnificence to which we
must cling as to a treasure, and not squander on our
way through life in the small coin of empty words,
or in exact and priggish argument.

GEORGE SAND,
Letter to Des Planches, 25 May 1866

3 December

We all are so deeply interconnected; we have no option but to love all. Be kind and do good for any one and that will be reflected. The ripples of the kind heart are the highest blessings of the Universe.

AMIT RAY, *Yoga and Vipassana*

4 December: *Hanukkah*

As you go on with your life, always remember the things that are good in you. They're your gifts. As long as you have these things, you'll find happiness, and you'll make the people around you happy.

GENKI KAWAMURA,
If Cats Disappeared From the World

5 December

Refuse to believe, and you shall indeed be right.
But believe, and again you shall be right, for you
shall save yourself. You make one or the other of two
possible universes true by your trust or mistrust –
both universes having been only maybes.

WILLIAM JAMES, Harvard speech, May 1895

6 December: *St Nicholas' Day*

And each day life will bestow more blessings
upon us if we are kind.

BHUWAN THAPALIYA

How could you show kindness this season?

7 December

There is no blessing like the breath of life.

LAILAH GIFTY AKITA

8 December

Yesterday is not ours to recover, but tomorrow is ours
to win or lose.

LYNDON B. JOHNSON,
Washington, 29 November 1963

9 December

Perhaps one of the only positive pieces of advice
that I was ever given was that supplied by an old
courtier who observed: only two rules really count.
Never miss an opportunity to relieve yourself;
never miss a chance to sit down and rest your feet.

EDWARD DUKE OF WINDSOR, *A King's Story*

10 December

Faith consists in believing when it is beyond the power of reason to believe.

VOLTAIRE, *Philosophical Dictionary*

11 December

What I dream of is an art of balance, of purity and serenity devoid of troubling or depressing subject matter – a soothing, calming influence on the mind, rather like a good armchair which provides relaxation from physical fatigue.

HENRI MATISSE, *Notes of a Painter*

12 December

We grow through our dreams. All great men and women
are dreamers. Some, however, allow their dreams to die.
You should nurse your dreams and protect them through
bad times and tough times to the sunshine and light
which always comes through.

WOODROW WILSON

13 December

There is an innocence in admiration; it is found in those to whom it has never yet occurred that they, too, might be admired some day.

FRIEDRICH NIETZSCHE, *Beyond Good and Evil*

14 December

Beautiful music is the art of the prophets that can calm the agitations of the soul; it is one of the most magnificent and delightful presents God has given us.

MARTIN LUTHER

15 December

He who is of calm and happy nature will hardly feel the pressure of age, but to him who is of an opposite disposition youth and age are equally a burden.

PLATO, *The Republic*

16 December

Until the day when God shall deign to reveal the future to man, all human wisdom is summed up in these two words: wait and hope.

ALEXANDRE DUMAS,
The Count of Monte Cristo

What are your favourite memories of Christmas? Which of these could you share with others?

17 December

Christmas is the spirit of giving without a thought of getting. It is happiness because we see joy in people. It is forgetting self and finding more time for others. It is discarding the meaningless and stressing the true values.

THOMAS S. MONSON, 'Christmas is Love', 2012

18 December

Our dead are never dead to us, until we have forgotten them.

GEORGE ELIOT, *Adam Bede*

19 December

Experience is simply the name we give our mistakes.

OSCAR WILDE, *The Picture of Dorian Grey*

20 December

I intend to live forever, or die trying.

GROUCHO MARX

21 December: *Winter Solstice*

We may have different religions, different languages,
different colored skin, but we all belong to one
human race.

KOFI ANNAN

22 December

As a well spent day brings happy sleep, so life well
used brings happy death.

LEONARDO DA VINCI, *Codex Trivulzianus*

What are your favourite songs from this time of year?

23 December

Success is getting what you want, happiness is
wanting what you get.

DALE CARNEGIE

24 December: *Christmas Eve*

May you never be too grown up to search the
skies on Christmas Eve.

ANONYMOUS

25 December: *Christmas Day*

I will honour Christmas in my heart, and try to keep it all the year. I will live in the Past, the Present, and the Future.

CHARLES DICKENS, *A Christmas Carol*

26 December: *Boxing Day*

God doesn't need my permission to change my life;
but he does need my cooperation. 'You can't get away from
yourself by moving from one place to another.'

ERNEST HEMINGWAY

27 December

I am finally learning really to live one day at a time and
to appreciate and be alert to the beautiful, marvel-filled,
albeit sometimes infuriating world around me.

'Beyond the Generation Gap', *Grapevine*, August 1985

28 December: *Bank Holiday*

The wound, is where the light enters you . . .

RUMI

29 December

In quietness and trust is your strength.

Isaiah 30.15

30 December

A sound judgment and a close application may
do more for you than the most brilliant talent.
In the ordinary business of life anything can be done
by industry which can be done by 'genius'; also many
things which 'genius', pure and simple, cannot do.
There is something for every youth within the reach
of industry which 'genius' alone can never win.

ORISON SWETT MARDEN, *The Optimistic Life*

31 December: *New Year's Eve*

The future is completely open and we are
writing it moment to moment.

PEMA CHÖDRÖN

Notes for December

ACKNOWLEDGEMENTS

What a blessing it has been to have the best team in the business! My sincere thanks to you all for believing in this book and working so hard to bring it to life.

Love and gratitude to Andy Lyon. Thanks for never dismissing my crazy ideas and for always offering plenty of encouragement. You're a dear friend!

Huge thanks to Ruth Roff, my editor, for putting up with my endless emails and changes! Your patience and guidance has been a Godsend.

Thanks to Purvi Gadia for all the positive energy and help in putting the book together.

Thanks also to Toni Michelle who has done wonders with all the illustrations. Sorry if I was too fussy!

Big thanks to Rhoda Hardie, Emily Short, Olivia Bromage, Linda De Angelis and Alex Orr for supplying the brilliant PR opportunities. Great to work with you.

A massive thanks to the entire team at Hodder & Stoughton who have worked so hard to make this book a success. I'm so grateful to Mayeule Huard for all the fab research, and to Mary Jane Greatrex, the copy editor, Caroline Priestly, the deputy art director, and Diana Talyanina, the senior production controller. Thanks also to 'eagle eyes' Gabrielle Mentjox for spotting all the little errors!

Love and thanks to all the other unsung publishing superheroes who help us fall in love with books.

Thanks also to my manager, Kathryn Nash.

Finally, my thanks to you for allowing this book to be a part of your life. I hope it brings comfort and joy in equal measure.

P.S. Don't feel bad if the first thing you do is turn to your birth date to read what the blessing says! Don't worry, everyone does it!

RAISING READERS
Books Build Bright Futures

Dear Reader,

We'd love your attention for one more page to tell you about the crisis in children's reading, and what we can all do.

Studies have shown that reading for fun is the **single biggest predictor of a child's future life chances** – more than family circumstance, parents' educational background or income. It improves academic results, mental health, wealth, communication skills, ambition and happiness.[1]

The number of children reading for fun is in rapid decline. Young people have a lot of competition for their time. In 2024, 1 in 10 children and young people in the UK aged 5 to 18 did not own a single book at home.[2]

Hachette works extensively with schools, libraries and literacy charities, but here are some ways we can all raise more readers:

- Reading to children for just 10 minutes a day makes a difference
- Don't give up if children aren't regular readers – there will be books for them!
- Visit bookshops and libraries to get recommendations
- Encourage them to listen to audiobooks
- Support school libraries
- Give books as gifts

There's a lot more information about how to encourage children to read on our website: **www.RaisingReaders.co.uk**

Thank you for reading.

hachette
UK

[1] OECD, '21st-Century Readers: Developing Literacy Skills in a Digital World', 2021, https://www.oecd.org/en/publications/21st-century-readers_a83d84cb-en.html

[2] National Literacy Trust, 'Book Ownership in 2024', November 2024, https://literacytrust.org.uk/research-services/research-reports/book-ownership-in-2024